Beholding Heavenly Light
Lessons from Christian Masterpieces

Beholding Heavenly Light

Lessons from Christian Masterpieces

James Thomas Angelidis

Beholding Heavenly Light:
Lessons from Christian Masterpieces

James Thomas Angelidis

www.jtangelidis.com

Copyright © 2021 by James Thomas Angelidis.

All rights reserved.

Reprinted with no revisions to literature 2023.

Cover Design:
Layout by James Thomas Angelidis.

Cover Image:
Arrangement and photograph by James Thomas Angelidis.

Author Image:
(On back cover and author bio page) Photograph by Eddie Manso.

"every scribe who has been trained for the kingdom of heaven is like a householder who brings out of his treasure what is new and what is old."

- Jesus Christ (Matthew 13:52, RSV)

AUTHOR BIO

James Thomas Angelidis has been awarded three university degrees and has authored and independently published several Christian books. These accomplishments helped him become a Professor of Christian Theology at Seton Hall University in South Orange, New Jersey. Discover James's works on his website at www.jtangelidis.com.

SPECIAL THANKS TO...

... Rev. Msgr. Thomas G. Guarino, who I first met when I was his student at Seton Hall University's Immaculate Conception Seminary School of Theology in South Orange, NJ. Fr. Guarino believed in me and helped make possible my position as Professor of Christian Theology at Seton Hall University. This book is the product of my work as Professor. Without Fr. Guarino, this book would never have been written. Fr. Guarino is a true friend and my brother in Christ Jesus. Thank you, Fr. Guarino.

... Rev. Protopresbyter Constantine (Costa) L. Sitaras, who I first met when I was a youth and who blessed me with the honor of working with him and the children at Saint Basil Academy in Garrison, NY. As I have grown to be a man, I have developed a strong relationship with our Lord and Savior Jesus Christ. I love Jesus with tears and a joyful heart. This is largely attributed to my Orthodox faith, the Orthodox Church and the Orthodox clergy. My relationship with Jesus has grown stronger with Fr. Costa's guidance. Thank you, Fr. Costa.

CONTENTS

PREFACE
- 13 -

MASTERPIECE: Saint Augustine's *The City of God*
TITLE OF EXPOSITION: Reintroducing Saint Augustine and His Masterpiece *The City of God*
- 15 -

MASTERPIECE: Dionysius the Areopagite's *The Celestial Hierarchy*
TITLE OF EXPOSITION: Celestial Hierarchy and the Angelic Method
- 55 -

MASTERPIECE: Saint Athanasius's *Life of Antony*
TITLE OF EXPOSITION: Saint Antony and the Way to Theosis
- 97 -

MASTERPIECE: Anonymously authored *The Way of a Pilgrim*
TITLE OF EXPOSITION: Praying Unceasingly as Holy Life
- 145 -

PREFACE

The four expositions in this book are based on my lessons as a University Professor of Christian Theology. I wrote the expositions during the 2020 Covid-19 coronavirus pandemic and posted them on my website. The four expositions are distinct from one another, and my writing styles are different, as well. However, they have common Christian themes, most significantly being theosis (deification, divinization - being made divine). In each exposition, I believe the examined Christian masterpiece's heavenly light shines through.

I was initially going to put the expositions in the chronological order of when the examined masterpieces were authored. However, when considering the content of the material, I realized it was more appropriate to begin with Saint Augustine's masterpiece *The City of God* because it literally sets the stage for the other expositions. Saint Augustine's masterpiece is like a spiritual map of the world, and it illustrates the dynamic of those who are in this present world – between those of the heavenly City of God and those of the earthly City of Man. The other masterpieces are about citizens who live in the heavenly city, and knowledge of the heavenly city would serve as a good introduction for the rest of the material. To not place the exposition about the heavenly city and the earthly city at the beginning and rather later on would be a distraction and disrupt the book as a whole. In fact, the exposition on Saint Augustine's masterpiece is the perfect way to begin this book because of its panoramic scope. Augustine's masterpiece provides context for the masterpieces that follow it. The second exposition is on Dionysius the Areopagite's masterpiece *The Celestial Hierarchy*, which is about holy angels who are the leader citizens of the heavenly city. The third exposition is on Saint Athanasius's masterpiece *Life of Antony*, which is about Saint Antony – one of the greatest saints and citizens of the heavenly city. The fourth and final exposition is on the anonymously authored masterpiece *The Way of a Pilgrim*, which is about a man who wandered around Russia learning about prayer as a citizen of the heavenly city. With the first exposition, the picture is broadest, and then the picture narrows with each following exposition until it reaches the final exposition on *The Way of a Pilgrim* where the main figure is most like us – though be certain that we can learn about ourselves from each masterpiece (that is their strength and great value).

    Working on this book brought me much joy, and I hope it brings you joy, as well.

With agape love in Christ Jesus,
James Thomas Angelidis

MASTERPIECE: Saint Augustine's *The City of God*

TITLE OF EXPOSITION: Reintroducing Saint Augustine and His Masterpiece *The City of God*

Description

For the 2020 Easter season, I was scheduled to lecture at the Metropolitan Cathedral of Saint John the Theologian in Tenafly, NJ. The event was cancelled because of the pandemic, but I posted my lecture for free on my website. The lecture is about rarely discussed, but relevant and significant ideas. I examine Saint Augustine's masterpiece *The City of God* with his lessons on the divided angels (holy versus wicked) and the corresponding two cities (heavenly City of God and earthly City of Man) that exist in our present world. I also examine human beings as citizens in the two cities, peace and war in the two cities, as well as eternal Salvation. Many of you may not come across these ideas, again, for many years. The literature could lead your soul away from suffering and inspire you to live a more holy life. It is worth reading. Enjoy and may God bless you.

Contents

+ Ethos Introduction of Author and Professor James Thomas Angelidis
+ About Saint Augustine
+ Divided Angels and Corresponding Two Cities
+ Human Beings as Citizens in the City of God and the City of Man
+ Peace and War in the Heavenly City and the Earthly City
+ Unto Ages of Ages
+ Concluding Remarks with Free Copies of My Book
  - *Young Ezekiel: A Life of Loves*

Work Cited

- Saint Augustine. *The City of God* (ed. and trans. by Marcus Dods). Project Gutenberg: https://www.gutenberg.org. Accessed 6-15-2018.

Ethos Introduction
[Tap on microphone to make sure it works]

Good evening friends... My name is James Thomas Angelidis, and I want to thank you for joining me today here at the Metropolitan Cathedral of Saint John the Theologian. I want to begin by saying I love this church. I was baptized in this church. I went to Sunday School in this church. And, I have been a regular parishioner in this church for much of my adult life. Standing here in front of you - my fellow brothers and sisters in Christ - brings me great joy and is a true honor. I love Jesus Christ very much, and I love His saints. Today, I will teach you what I have learned from my favorite saint - Saint Augustine. However, before I begin my lesson, I want to take about 5 minutes to express why you can trust me as a reliable source of information.

Credibility is important. As learners, we all have to know the sources of information from which we are learning. It is one of the first things I look into when I choose a new book to read. I see who the author is and if he or she seems to know what he or she is talking about. I see if the person has strong credentials. So, let me speak briefly about why you can trust me as a reliable source.

I have 3 university degrees. I received my first bachelor's degree from **Boston University** where I was most interested in philosophy. I was always a thoughtful person, and philosophy encouraged me to think more deeply. I remember my very first class at Boston University was about ancient Greek Philosopher Plato's *The Republic*. I was mesmerized by Plato - and his book *The Republic* is a classic of western literature. The ancient Greeks were insightful.

Philosophy was a major interest of mine, and I treasured philosophical literature, but it was not my passion. It would take a few more years for me to discover my passion. Philosophy gave me direction, but the **study of religion** ended up being my passion. I found answers in the world religions. I studied all the world religions to find out the meaning of life. I wanted to know life's purpose and how I could excel and be the greatest that I could be. I was drawn to words like immortality and eternity - and all these positive words pointed to Almighty God. He is the Greatest Good that exists, so I was compelled to read, study and learn about God. After I graduated from BU, I spent every day for the next 2 years studying the sacred scriptures of the 6 major world religions. I studied 17 sacred texts in total. I consider this period the beginning of my adulthood. In the end, of all the religions, I found the highest truths in Christianity. As I have gotten older, the truths of the Christian

Faith have revealed themselves more clearly in my life. My faith in Jesus Christ has grown stronger as an adult. I have found that Jesus is the way and the truth to immortality, eternity and God.

During this time, I also worked a bunch of jobs and lived life in the world for a bit. With money I saved, I decided to invest in myself, and at the age of 24, I **backpacked through Europe** for 2 months. In 60 days, I visited 28 cities in 11 countries and saw nearly all the major sites. I took this adventure by myself, and it taught me how to survive on my own.

After the trip, I worked some other jobs, and then I returned to school for a second bachelor's degree. This time from **Montclair State University** where I majored in the world religions. I did this to learn from knowledgeable professors about God and God's Ways.

Because of my relationship with God and my desire to do good things in this world, I worked at a children's home for 9 years called **Saint Basil Academy** in upstate New York. There, I helped raise children who were in need. For different reasons, the children's parents could not take care of them, so we raised them.

During this time, I continued to read about God and God's Ways on my own. I returned to formal academic education and got a third university degree - this time a master's degree from **Seton Hall University's Seminary** where I devoted myself to the teachings of Jesus Christ.

With all this education and my desire to share what I learned and to share what transformed my life, **I became an author.** I have written and published 5 books. They all have to do with Jesus Christ. I wrote and illustrated a children's book for 7 to 9-year-olds which is based on the kids I worked with at the home, and it teaches Gospel lessons. I wrote a 2nd book that is an allegory where, through the life of a young man, I tell a story about the four forms of love: storge, philia, eros, agape. I wrote a 3rd book with scholarly Christin material for college students. My 4th book contains mature Christian theology for adults. And, my 5th book is an anthology of the previous 4 - which is over 500 pages, and which represents 15 years of study and 10 years of writing. I wrote all these books for the world and to share with the world about what saved me. Plus, I have a website on the internet.

Because of what is inside my books and because I excelled as a graduate student at Seton Hall University's Seminary, I was hired by Seton Hall University as an **Adjunct Professor** to teach Christian Theology to undergraduates. My primary course is called Christian Belief and Thought, and in it, I highlight the teachings of Jesus Christ as well as

His saints. We begin with Christianity's origins and journey to modern times. I have also had the honor to teach a course on Eastern Orthodox Christianity - which was a wonderful experience.

Today's Lecture is a condensed version of what I teach my students in my Christian Belief and Thought course at Seton Hall University. I spend 3 class sessions on Saint Augustine and his masterpiece *The City of God*. Today, I will highlight the most striking elements from the text in less than 40 minutes.

[Identify distributed handout] ... I would like to point out that there is a handout - in yellow - on your tables. It includes an outline of the lecture and valuable passages from Saint Augustine's masterpiece *The City of God*. For the next few minutes, I will talk a bit about Saint Augustine.

About Saint Augustine

I want to confess that Jesus Christ is my Lord and Savior. Along with God, Jesus is number one in my life. I have structured my life around Him and His teachings. No one else compares. However, of all other human beings to walk the earth, I have learned the most from Saint Augustine. I consider him my dearest friend. No other saint has taught me more.

Saint Augustine was the Bishop of Hippo in North Africa and died in AD 430. In the Eastern Orthodox Church, he is a saint, and in the Western Catholic Church, he is not only a saint but also a Doctor of the Church. Since Christianity's emergence, nearly 2000 years ago, only 36 saints have been given this title and honor in the Catholic Church [as of 2015]. He is, perhaps, the most influential of the Western Church Fathers. People in the Eastern Orthodox Church have mixed opinions about him. However, Saint Augustine is without doubt a giant in the Christian world. I once visited an Orthodox monastery, which houses the most Orthodox members of our Church, and an erudite monk told me that Augustine is indeed one of our greatest saints. 20th century Orthodox Christian convert and scholar Jaroslav Pelikan said Western theology's history since the 500s is "'a series of footnotes' to Augustine" (1971).

Saint Augustine's **two most famous works** are his autobiography called *Confessions* and his apologetic work *The City of God*.

His book **Confessions** is the first ever written Western autobiography. It is a story of infancy, youth, maturity and adulthood. Augustine wrote about his development, which culminated in him renouncing his sinful life and converting to Christianity. It is an honest confession of one's life that has testimonial meditations and prayerfulness like in the Old Testament's Book of Psalms.

Augustine's **The City of God** is apologetic literature with two distinct evolving halves. The first half, Books 1-10, is negative apologetics and is a defense or argument against pagans who asserted that Christians were responsible for the downfall of the Roman Empire. The second half, Books 11-22, which is of most interest to us, is positive apologetics and becomes a theological history of the universe and humankind. It is a defense of the true nature of the Christian Church and the destiny of its people who make up the heavenly City of God, which is unlike and contrary to the earthly City of Man. 20th century Catholic Christian author and monk Thomas Merton said, "The City of God is the autobiography of the Church written by the most Catholic of her great saints" (1950). Tonight, I will highlight for you some powerful theology that is in this book *The City of God*.

Let us begin with the...

Divided Angels
and Corresponding Two Cities

(point to poster board)

The subject of angels takes up more than 5% of Saint Augustine's 900-page book. So, that is more than 45 pages on angels.

Some people may question **if angels really exist**. And I believe that the confirmation from the Holy Scriptures and the Divine Liturgy are enough. Angels are mentioned throughout the Old Testament as well as throughout the New Testament. Jesus himself refers to angels, and during our church services, we pray to the Lord "For an angel of peace, a faithful guide, a guardian of our souls and bodies." I have no doubt that angels exist. I believe angels and demons influence our lives on a regular basis.

With Book/Chapter Eleven begins the second part of Saint Augustine's masterpiece, which treats the two cities - the heavenly and the earthly. These two cities were formed originally by the separation of the good and bad angels. I will highlight key passages from Augustine's masterpiece so you can begin to see what this great saint saw and knew.

In Book Eleven, Augustine begins by declaring the **authority of Scripture**. He says:
> Scripture, which excels all the writings of all nations by its divine authority. (11.1)

Then, he quotes the Old Testament references to the City of God. He says:
> For there it is written, "Glorious things are spoken of thee, O city of God." And in another psalm we read, "Great is the Lord, and greatly to be praised in the city of our God, in the mountain of His holiness, increasing the joy of the whole earth." … From these and similar testimonies, all of which it were tedious to cite, we have learned that there is a city of God, and its Founder has inspired us with a love which makes us covet its citizenship. (11.1)

Augustine explains that:
> **the two cities (the earthly and the heavenly, to wit) … are in this present world commingled, and as it were entangled together**. (11.1)

These two cities are not separated by borders, walls or territory. They exist spiritually; although, they can manifest physically and be perceived by our senses.

Try to understand that the heavenly City of God exists in this present world that we live in. When you are in the mall or are walking down the street to the coffee shop or are in any public place, the cities are there - both cities, the earthly as well as the heavenly. The world is a mysterious and mystical place and the two cities both exist in this world in a commingled and entangled manner. Both cities have shape and form in this present world. It is a hard lesson, but if you are aware of it and pay attention, you will see the truth of Saint Augustine's claims. And, hopefully, you will desire and choose to live in the heavenly city.

Both cities exist right now in this world and came into existence and began with the divided angels. Augustine says:
> the **foundations of these two cities** were originally laid, in the difference that arose among the angels. (11.1)

God is the Creator who created everything, including the angels who are the first citizens of the two cities. Augustine begins with the Book of Genesis and explains that though not explicitly stated in the Genesis Creation story, angels were indeed made by God as mentioned elsewhere in Scripture. He provides citations, including from the Book of Psalms. (11.9)

Saint Augustine dug very deep to unpack Scripture. Human beings have to sometimes unpack Scripture to unearth and reveal the truth. This task must be done by the greatest and most informed, and Saint Augustine is one of the best. The saint also cites the

Book of Job and works back to Genesis. He points out:
> God says, "When the stars were made, the angels praised me with a loud voice."[459] The angels therefore existed before the stars; and the stars were made the fourth day. (11.9)

The great saint explains:
> There is no question, then, that if the angels are included in the works of God during these six days, they are that light which was called "Day," and whose unity Scripture signalizes by calling that day not the "first day," but "one day."[460] For the second day, the third, and the rest are not other days; but the same "one" day is repeated to complete the number six or seven, so that there should be knowledge both of God's works and of His rest. (11.9)

Saint Augustine explains angels were made on day one as that light which was called Day. I encourage you to consider the **truth of God creating the universe**. When God created and there was one day, a second day, a third day - that amount of time is a reflection of God's efforts. A day could be 24 hours or a million years in God's timeframe of completion. Saint Peter explains, "do not ignore this one fact, beloved, that with the Lord one day is as a thousand years, and a thousand years as one day" (2 Peter 3:8). This concept of time is something to think about.

God's work in time is different than our understanding of time. In addition, I want you to consider the Creation story as theological wisdom that is as relevant as scientific theory. The Creation story teaches truths, and we can learn from it. The Creation story is just as valuable as scientific theory. Science does not have all the answers. Science suggests the universe began with a big bang moment, but it confesses that it cannot explain what was before that moment. And, the origins of humankind as well as the origins of life itself remain a mystery to the scientific community. The theory of evolution suggests that we human beings - in all our complexity - evolved from microscopic cells similar to bacteria. That is a bold conclusion - that we evolved from bacteria-like organisms. Remember, this is theory, hypothesis, speculation, guesswork. Scientific theories are merely philosophies based on data which are often replaced by new scientific theories without indisputable conclusiveness. I am not saying that science is not useful. Science has value. We can learn from science, but just remember, science does not have all the answers. If living things are similar in any way, perhaps it was God's design for living things to be similar. In truth, we may never be satisfied with our understanding of how the universe, life and humanity began. The origin of existence is mysterious, and we can continue to ask questions as long as we do not disregard the belief that God is Creator as expressed in the Bible. The point is - do not dismiss God and the wisdom of Scripture. Let us continue with Scripture and see what we can learn from the great Saint Augustine's insight into the Genesis Creation narrative.

Augustine explains that **God - with His unchangeable Wisdom - is Eternal Light** and that angels were created by God to be light as well - physically, intellectually and spiritually. They were created when God said, "Let there be light, and there was light." And, the angels of light are called "Day." Those **angels that turned away from God became darkness.** God divided the light from the darkness and darkness is evil because it is without light. Augustine explains:

> For when God said, "Let there be light, and there was light," if we are justified in understanding in this light the creation of the angels, then certainly they were created partakers of the eternal light which is the unchangeable Wisdom of God, by which all things were made, and whom we call the only-begotten Son of God; so that they, being illumined by the Light that created them, might themselves become light and be called "Day," in participation of that unchangeable Light and Day which is the Word of God, by whom both themselves and all else were made. "The true Light, which lighteth every man that cometh into the world,"[461]—this

> Light lighteth also every pure angel, that he may be light not in himself, but in God; from whom if an angel turn away, he becomes impure, as are all those who are called unclean spirits, and are no longer light in the Lord, but darkness in themselves, being deprived of the participation of Light eternal. For evil has no positive nature; but the loss of good has received the name "evil." (11.9)

Each fallen angel is an apostate, meaning one who renounces or abandons, a traitor. Augustine explains:
> Wherefore, though light and darkness are to be taken in their literal signification in these passages of Genesis in which it is said, "God said, Let there be light, and there was light," and "God divided the light from the darkness," yet, for our part, we understand these two societies of angels,—the one enjoying God, the other swelling with pride; the one to whom it is said, "Praise ye Him, all His angels,"[512] the other whose prince says, "All these things will I give Thee if Thou wilt fall down and worship me;"[513] the one blazing with the holy love of God, the other reeking with the unclean lust of self-advancement. (11.33)

Both societies of angels are by nature good, but they are distinguished by **upright and depraved wills**. Augustine explains:

> These two angelic communities, then, dissimilar and contrary to one another, the one both by nature good and by will upright, the other also good by nature but by will depraved, as they are exhibited in other and more explicit passages of holy writ, so I think they are spoken of in this book of Genesis under the names of light and darkness... (11.33)

God separated the fallen angels who became darkness from the upright angels who remained light. We do the same with people who possess light and darkness. We can sense light and darkness in people. Augustine cites Apostle Paul who says:
> "Ye are all the children of light, and [Pg 479] the children of the day: we are not of the night, nor of darkness." (11.33)

People are of light and darkness, as Apostle Paul says, and if people can be light or darkness, it is certainly more true for holy angels and evil angels. We know evil angels as **demons**. These demons are as real as the holy angels. People often refer to them in common dialogue. One person might ask another, "How is your friend doing?" And a response could be, "He is having a tough time. He is battling his demons." Drug abuse, forms of addiction, depression and mental illness are all from the influence of demons. We all struggle with and battle demons.

Saint Augustine explains there are two cities - each with angels and people - in this present world. A holy city with good angels and good people versus a wicked city with bad angels and bad people. (12.1)

Next, Augustine, while distinguishing between the good angels versus the bad angels, further explains that **God is Good and created everything good**. All angels started out good. Good angels remained good with good wills and good desires. Evil angels turned away from God believing in their own power with selfish pride. Augustine says:

> That the contrary propensities in good and bad angels have arisen, not from a difference in their nature and origin, since God, the good Author and Creator of all essences, created them both, but from a difference in their wills and desires, it is impossible to doubt. While some stedfastly continued in that which was the common good of all, namely, in God Himself, and in His eternity, truth, and love; others, being enamoured rather of their own power, as if they could be their own good, lapsed to this private good of their own, from that higher and beatific good which was common to all, and, bartering the lofty dignity of eternity for the inflation of pride, the most assured verity for the slyness of vanity,

uniting love for factious partisanship, they became proud, deceived, envious. (12.1)

Augustine teaches that **good versus bad is defined by adherence to God** because God is the Source of Good. Created angels and human beings are only blessed if they adhere to their Creator who without leads to misery. The only true unchangeable blessed Good is God who the created must adhere to for their own well-being. (12.1)

Then, Augustine teaches that the **rational soul is superior** to other created things because it can recognize God and can participate with God. Although, it is true other created things cannot suffer the misery of hell. It is also true they cannot enjoy the blessedness of heaven. The blessedness of the rational soul is within its power to choose. (12.1)

Angels were created to adhere to God. Adhering to God is why they were created. The vice of the evil angels is that they did not remain in their proper nature in fellowship with God. (12.1)

This idea of light versus darkness is probably familiar to many of you. I'm sure it sounds familiar. For example, in popular culture, it appears in the *Star Wars* films with the opposite sides of the Force. *Star Wars* has value for the youth because it contains truths. Noticeably, Darth Vader is the most popular character in the franchise, and he was heavily influenced by the dark side. You will notice the influence of the dark side elsewhere in popular culture, as well. Some people today like to glorify evil. The villain often appears heroic and many people envy his corrupt power and want to be like him and thereby root for him on television and in film. We see this with comic book villains and with gangsters. This is exactly what the devil wants. He wants you to think it's acceptable and desirable to be bad. The theme of light versus darkness appears throughout human cultures and Augustine has written about it in a big way within a Biblical context through the two societies of angels.

Next, we will investigate...

Human Beings
as Citizens in the City of God and the City of Man

(point to poster board)

The angels of light and the angels of darkness were the beginning of two very real cities in this present world - the heavenly City of God and the earthly City of Man. With the angels, there exist men and women.

Human beings and angels have a special relationship and together they inhabit the cities. I have just highlighted Augustine's scholarship on the angels. Now, let us focus on humankind. I will highlight Augustine's scholarship on humankind's origin and nature and its citizenships in the heavenly City of God and the earthly City of Man.

In Book Thirteen, we learn about humankind's penalty and punishment. Augustine explains:
> death is penal, and had its **origin in Adam's sin**. (13)

The first punishment for the transgression of our first parents Adam and Eve is that they felt shame because of their **sexual desires** and could not control their flesh. As a result of being their children, we human beings have inherited this trial. Augustine cites Galatians 5:17 by Apostle Paul, which says:
> Then began the flesh to lust against the Spirit. (13.13)

Augustine shows us that there is a special likeness between angels and humankind. Both possess the power of **free will**. In each, the fallen fell for the same reason because they chose to fall with their free wills. He points out:
> man ... fell by the choice of his own will. (13.14)

Augustine explains **man's current corrupt state,** which began with our first parents Adam and Eve. He says,

> God ... created man upright; but man, being of his own will corrupted, and justly condemned, begot corrupted and condemned children ... And thus, from the bad use of free will, there originated the whole train of evil, which, with its concatenation of miseries, convoys the human race from its depraved origin, as from a corrupt root, on to the destruction of the second death, which has no end, those only being excepted who are freed by the grace of God. (13.14)

Next is particularly important because Augustine teaches:

> What it is to **live according to man**, and what to **live according to God**. (14.4)

The great saint teaches that man who lives according to himself without God is acting like the devil. We should live according to God and not ourselves because God is the only Truth. Living according to anything other than God, including ourselves, is untrustworthy. And, living in the truth is better than living in any lie. When we sin, we are living according to a lie because all sin is a lie. Sin is tempting, but in the end, it makes us more miserable because we are abandoning God who is the only source of good and true happiness. (14.4)

Then, Augustine acutely identifies the **life of flesh versus the life of spirit**:
> because some live according to the flesh and others according to the spirit there have arisen two diverse and conflicting cities, we might equally well have said, "because some live according to man, others according to God." (14.4)

Earthly citizens live according to the flesh and man, while heavenly citizens live according to the spirit and God. Man is flesh, carnal and animal. However, he also has the Spirit of God in him which teaches him the truth of his nature. The Spirit in him teaches. The animal in him makes him ignorant. We are meant to rise above our animal and be spiritual. We should live not according to man but according to God. Man is flesh and soul. We cannot escape our animal, but if we follow God and live in the Spirit, we can become holy like God, we can attain union with God and become gods. In Orthodoxy, this is known as **theosis**. (14.4)

Augustine explains the righteous are blessed, but even they are not completely happy until they reach eternal life because that is what they seek. He points out:

> Of true blessedness, which this present life cannot enjoy. (14.25)

Augustine provides an excellent expression of the **human struggle**. The struggle for life, but also wanting it to end. He says:
> what man is at present able to live as he wishes, when it is not in his power so much as to live? He wishes to live, he is compelled to die. (14.25)

He then explains that a blessed man loves his life but nonetheless looks to eternity where the blessedness is eternal. (14.25)

Then, the great saint talks about **God's providence** - that is God's protective care, will and wisdom in the universe. He explains:
> Of the angels and men who sinned, and that their wickedness did not disturb the order of God's providence. (14.27)

Augustine wants us to know that God is Wise, All-Powerful and in total control. He explains:
> [God] is able to make good use not only of the good, but also of the wicked. (14.27)

Augustine is not afraid to confront the most difficult questions. He writes:

why should not God have **permitted him [Satan] to tempt the first man**? (14.27)

Augustine's answer is that God allowed Satan to tempt the first man to see if man would remain loyal to God. It was a test of loyalty. He says:
> if he [man] looked to God for help, man's goodness should defeat the angel's wickedness; but if by proud self-pleasing he abandoned God, his Creator and Sustainer, he should be conquered. If his will remained upright, through leaning on God's help, he should be rewarded; if it became wicked, by forsaking God, he should be punished. (14.27)

Augustine explains that our blessings are the result of God's power; however, our downfall is our own doing. He says:
> it was not in man's power, even in Paradise, to live as he ought without God's help; but it was in his power to live wickedly... (14.27)

Then, Augustine restates the question. He asks:
> why should He [God] not have suffered him [man] to be tempted by an angel who hated and envied him? (14.27)

Augustine provides a second answer to why God allowed the devil to tempt the first man by highlighting the saints. He says:

> He [God] foresaw that by the man's seed, aided by divine grace, this same devil himself should be conquered, to the greater glory of the saints. (14.27)

An adjacent answer to why God allows sin is to show us our weakness and the power of God's good grace. (14.27)

Augustine takes time to identify and clarify:
> the nature of the two cities, the earthly and the heavenly. (14.28)

In a core teaching of his masterpiece, he says,
> Accordingly, **two cities have been formed by two loves**: the earthly by the love of self, even to the contempt of God; the heavenly by the love of God, even to the contempt of self. The former, in a word, glories in itself, the latter in the Lord. For the one seeks glory from men; but the greatest glory of the other is God, the witness of conscience. The one lifts up its head in its own glory; the other says to its God, "Thou art my glory, and the lifter up of mine head." ... [earthly] are ruled by the love of ruling ... [heavenly] serve one another in love... (14.28)

Then, he provides a description of citizens in the **earthly city**, even their best, who live to benefit themselves and give glory to themselves. (14.28)

Then, he provides a description of citizens in the **heavenly city**. He explains:
> But in the other city there is no human wisdom, but only godliness, which offers due worship to the true God, and looks for its reward in the society of the saints, of holy angels as well as holy men, "that God may be all in all." (14.28)

As I have shown you, the two cities have origins with the angels. Then, God created humankind as depicted with the story of Adam and Eve. The growth and progress of the two cities are described further in Scripture with Adam and Eve's descendants and continue to present day.

Let us continue with…

Peace and War
in the Heavenly City
and the Earthly City

(point to poster board)

Book Nineteen's argument is concerned with:
> the end of the two cities, the earthly and the heavenly... Augustine reviews the opinions of the philosophers regarding the Supreme Good, and their vain efforts to make for themselves a happiness in this life; and, while he refutes these, he takes occasion to show what the peace and happiness belonging to the heavenly city, or the **people of Christ**, are both now and hereafter. (19)

Here, Augustine makes clear that the citizens of the heavenly City of God are, in fact, the people of Christ.

Saint Augustine provides us with insight into the lives of the saints. I find comfort and hope in his words, and I believe you will, as well, because he tells us that **life is hard for everyone** - including God's elect. Not even the saints in the heavenly City of God are free from demons. We all struggle in this world. We all battle demons. The difference between most people and the saints is that the saints know how to endure. Augustine writes about:
> The reward prepared for the saints after they have endured the trial of this life. (19.10)

He explains:
> But not even the saints and faithful worshippers of the one true and most high

God are safe from the manifold temptations and deceits of the demons. (19.10)

However, the saints will be gifted with eternal blessedness. Here, a good life is mere misery compared to that final felicity - that final happiness. He says the saints will be given:
> gifts not only good, but eternal. (19.10)

He explains:
> There the virtues shall no longer be struggling against any vice or evil, but shall enjoy the reward of victory, the eternal peace which no adversary shall disturb. This is the final blessedness, this the ultimate consummation, the unending end. Here, indeed, we are said to be blessed when we have such peace as can be enjoyed in a good life; but such blessedness is mere misery compared to that final felicity. (19.10)

The great saint talks about the **power of virtue** and that virtue helps when life is easy and when life is hard. Virtue makes:
> good use of good and evil things. (19.10)

He explains that **peace is the goal** and final end of the City of God. Just as we wish R.I.P. (Rest In Peace) to someone who has died, so, too, is it the desired end for the City of God. Even Jerusalem means "Vision of Peace." The Supreme Good is peace with eternal life. The wicked do not have eternal life, but an eternal existence of punishment that lacks life. Therefore, the supreme good is not eternity, but eternal life and peace. Peace is a good so great that we cherish it in this world and look forward to it in the next. (19.11)

Augustine then investigates the difference and relationship between the **heavenly and earthly cities when understanding peace**. He examines:
> What produces peace, and what discord, between the heavenly and earthly cities. (19.17)

He explains:
> The earthly city, which does not live by faith, seeks an earthly peace, and the end it proposes, in the well-ordered concord of civic obedience and rule, is the combination of men's wills to attain the things which are helpful to this life. The heavenly city, or rather the part of it which sojourns on earth and lives by faith, makes use of this peace only because it must, until this mortal condition which necessitates it shall pass away. (19.17)

There is a point of **harmony between the two cities** in that the citizens of the heavenly city obey the laws of the earthly city to maintain mortal life - which is a goal shared by the earthly city, as well. But, the earthly city has many idols and gods that are worshiped; while the heavenly city worships only the One Almighty God. Therefore, the two cities are in conflict over laws regarding idolatry and worship, and the heavenly faces persecution from the earthly for not being like it. Nonetheless, the multitude of Christians and God Himself safeguard the heavenly city. The heavenly city welcomes diversity in every form as long as it does not hinder the worship of Almighty God. The heavenly city desires peace with the earthly city as long as the earthly does not injure the heavenly's faith in God. The heavenly city longs for peace for all under Almighty God, and when this does happen, this mortal life will be replaced by eternal life. (19.17)

Both cities treasure peace, but their attempts to achieve peace are **handled in different ways**. Peace is so sweet that even the corrupt city of man prizes it. But - I emphasize - peace for the selfish city of man is hard to accomplish because everyone has their own self interests. Everyone is looking out for themselves and not each other. It desires order, but in its nature it is disorganized. The City of Man is filled with chaos as we see in the world and on the television news. In the City of God, everyone is united under one God. The City of God treasures peace, as well. Peace is its ultimate goal, but the heavenly city knows the peace it enjoys in this life is not permanent and so it looks to the afterlife and peace with God where it is everlasting. (19.17)

Everyone in both the heavenly and earthly cities desires happiness and so Saint Augustine reveals what is true happiness and blessedness. He identifies the importance and **necessity of hope** in order to attain these goods, and no one is more blessed than the saints. He concludes that:
> the saints are in this life blessed in hope. (19.20)

And, hope, remember, is one of the three theological virtues, along with faith and love, which make possible happiness and peace.

The great saint identifies the value of hope in true happiness and true blessedness. The key insight is that:
> the happiness of this life, without the hope of what is beyond, is but a false happiness and profound misery. For the true blessings of the soul are not now enjoyed. (19.20)

When earthly peace is shared, there is harmony between the two cities. And, the people of God are directed by the Apostles and Prophets to pray for the earthly people who are synonymous with Babylon - the ancient city known for materialism and self-interest. This way those in the heavenly city can enjoy peace with those in the earthly city since the two cities are commingled and entangled together. (19.26)

The peace found in eternity cannot be fully understood in this present life. Augustine contends:
> That the peace of those who serve God cannot in this mortal life be apprehended in its perfection. (19.27)

Peace for the heavenly citizens in this life is **more of a non-negative than a positive**. This insight of Augustine's is very powerful and enlightening. He explains:
> the peace which we enjoy in this life, whether common to all or peculiar to ourselves, is rather the solace of our misery than the positive enjoyment of felicity. Our very righteousness, too, though true in so far as it has respect to the true good, is yet in this life of such a kind that it consists rather in the remission of sins than in the perfecting of virtues. (19.27)

Augustine cites the Lord's Prayer - the Our Father - as the City of God's prayer, which it uses to overcome sin and evil. (19.27)

Our mortal condition is filled with struggle. Augustine explains that:

the vices do not submit without a struggle…
[and that a man's] peace is not full so long as
he is at war with his vices. (19.27)

We all struggle, so we need God. And we pray to
God for mercy and grace. Only proud people do not
pray. God loves humility. (19.27)

The following is a description of the **final peace - the
Supreme Good**. It is something to look forward to.
This is a glimpse into eternal life. It is a beautiful
description of eternal life and peace articulated
through reason. Augustine writes:
> But, in that final peace to which all our
> righteousness has reference, and for the sake
> of which it is maintained, as our nature shall
> enjoy a sound immortality and incorruption,
> and shall have no more vices, and as we shall
> experience no resistance either from ourselves
> or from others, it will not be necessary that
> reason should rule vices which no longer
> exist, but God shall rule the man, and the soul
> shall rule the body, with a sweetness and
> facility suitable to the felicity of a life which
> is done with bondage. And this condition shall
> there be eternal, and we shall be assured of its
> eternity; and thus the peace of this blessedness
> and the blessedness of this peace shall be the
> supreme good. (19.27)

Next, Augustine describes **eternal death and hell for the wicked**. It is a scary description. A fate I wish on no one. He explains that there is a terrible war within the wicked in hell. As a frame of reference to this hell, he describes the strife and conflict we face within ourselves in this life and compares it to hell where a most bitter pain, torment and war is constant, never ending and without relief. (19.28)

Let us continue with…

Unto Ages of Ages

(point to poster board)

Book Twenty-two is the last chapter of Saint Augustine's masterpiece:
> This book treats of the end of the City of God, that is to say, of the eternal happiness of the saints; the faith of the resurrection of the body is established and explained; and the work concludes by showing how the saints, clothed in immortal and spiritual bodies, shall be employed. (22)

Augustine explains that the **true eternity** of the City of God will indeed be without end. And not to be mistaken with re-emerging generations of humankind as many people may intellectualize. This is the promise God has revealed in Scripture. (22.1)

Then, Augustine illustrates, **again, the creation of angels and men** as previously expressed. In brief, he explains that God did not deny or deprive angels and people the power of free will. We are not puppets. We have free will. However, many have misused it and brought evil upon themselves through their disobedience. We were made to be good. The darkness in demons and people shows this because of their distance from God who without is misery. People have the same power of free will as the angels. God allowed the misuse of free will because He knew He could make a greater good out of the evil - with a reward for those who chose good in a heavenly city that would have a greater and more overflowing population than before the wicked angels fell. (22.1)

Citizens in the City of God recognize and receive **Jesus Christ as Savior**. Augustine writes:
> Of the miseries and ills to which the human race is justly exposed through the first sin, and from which none can be delivered save by Christ's grace. (22.22)

We all descend from generations that began from Adam and Eve. We inherit the hard life given to us by our first parents. Augustine discusses the wrong doings that make life terrible for the wicked. We learn wickedness from previous generations. Without God, we would fall into sin constantly by choice. However, we can be saved by Jesus Christ. The name Jesus, in Hebrew, is Yeshua, which means Savior. That is his destiny. He fulfills his destiny as Savior for our benefit. Through Jesus, we are saved from misery and hell. (22.22)

Augustine teaches that people are aided in this life by **God's grace**, which is given to them in proportion to their faith. He also talks about philosophy and God's grace. And, that the true philosophy this world's sages seek is agreed by all to have come from God's grace. (22.22)

Augustine recognizes that we all struggle, but good people have different struggles than those who are bad. He explains that the war and struggle in good men is upon their vices. He explains how the passions of flesh and the Spirit battle each other … (22.23) … Then, he identifies the ways good men struggle. Sometimes, we win those battles, but those victories are not due to our own strength but rather God's grace through Jesus Christ. There is no struggle in heaven for those who make it through this troubled life with God and Jesus Christ.

In the section before the last of Augustine's masterpiece, he discusses the **beatific vision** of God

... (22.29) ... He explains how in the next life, we will see God as He is - everywhere and in all things. Augustine explains how we may behold God and be in His presence. In the next life, all will be good, and nothing will be hidden. Thoughts and hearts will be visible. And, all will praise God in His Glory.

Augustine concludes his masterpiece with insight regarding:
> the eternal felicity of the city of God, and of the perpetual Sabbath. (22.30)

There is a **key connection I want you to make**. This connection is key to understanding the importance and power of Saint Augustine's theology. The great saint wants us to understand and live in the City of God and Jesus Christ wants us to understand and live in the Kingdom of God. And, I tell you that **with the City begins the Kingdom**. If you understand that the City of God takes place in this present world, you will be more prepared to see the Kingdom of God on this planet. To be subjects in the Kingdom of God - that is God's Kingdom of Heaven - is what Jesus Christ wanted for us and it begins with us now. Jesus says in the Lord's Prayer - also known as the Our Father - "Thy Kingdom come, Thy will be done, on earth as it is in heaven." Jesus wants God's Kingdom of Heaven on earth. And, if we can make the connection between the City and the Kingdom, we will be closer to completing Jesus's vision and bring heaven to earth.

Concluding Remarks

There are two more things I would like to say before we end tonight.

One.
I encourage you to take the distributed handout with you because it contains valuable passages from Saint Augustine's masterpiece.

And, Two.
As a gift from me to you, I have copies of my book *Young Ezekiel: A Life of Loves*. Tonight, the book is free. For you to know what the book is about, allow me to read the back cover to you. This is a description of what is inside the book: [[pick up book from pile and read from it.]]

YOUNG EZEKIEL: A LIFE OF LOVES

> What is love?
> Can you describe it?
> Do you love your parents, friends, romantic partner and God in the same way?

In the English language, we use the word love in all these relationships, but the ancient Greeks - the first western philosophers - tried to capture, pinpoint and distinguish the different forms of love with four words: storge, philia, eros, agape.

In *Young Ezekiel: A Life of Loves*, Ezekiel will tell you about his life and loves. Though his life is unique, his relationships are like ours and, maybe, through his story, you will learn about yourself and the loves in your life.

So, the book is about a young man's life and through his story, you can enjoyably learn about the four forms of love: storge, philia, eros and agape. With Holy Week here, if you would like, you can begin with the chapter on agape, which describes Jesus's selfless self-sacrificial love. Most of the chapter takes place on Great Friday and the main character learns about the meaning of Jesus's agape love for us. The book ends with the main character celebrating Easter and our Risen Lord. Christ is Risen! - he announces. Tonight, this book is free. Enjoy! God bless! And thank you!

MASTERPIECE: Dionysius the Areopagite's *The Celestial Hierarchy*

TITLE OF EXPOSITION: Celestial Hierarchy and the Angelic Method

Description

The most influential and respected Christian document on angels, Dionysus the Areopagite's *The Celestial Hierarchy* is a masterpiece. Celestial means heavenly. Hierarchy means ranking. And, the masterpiece identifies the angelic method. In this exposition, you will learn how angels operate in Heaven and how this knowledge can lead you to theosis (divinization) and God. Enjoy and may God bless you.

Contents

+ Introduction
+ *The Celestial Hierarchy* Analysis
+ Conclusion
+ Work Cited

Introduction

Who are the angels? Some people think angels are fictional characters, others think they are physical people, and still others think they are something more spiritual. The word angel is derived from the Greek and Latin and translates into messenger. The term denotes their works. Angels are messengers of God. The word has been used for ordinary messengers, prophets and priests. However, it is primarily attributed to heavenly intelligences who God employs to fulfill His will in the world. They are not treated as a specific subject in the Bible, but their presence and works as guides and guardians are visible throughout. They are spirits, like the souls in men. However, when they appear to human beings, they usually take on human form, so there is a special relationship between them and humankind. In Scripture, they are usually physically described as men dressed in white. In art, angels have wings. Angels and saints are God's ultimate servants, and both have halos in art. The halo represents holiness.

Angels and saints share the same space in Heaven with God.

In the literary masterpiece the *Divine Comedy* by Dante Alighieri, there is a beautiful description of Heaven that was influenced by *The Celestial Hierarchy*, which is the focus of this exposition. Unfortunately, most people are only familiar with Dante's *Inferno* and are not aware that it is a part of a trilogy that includes *Purgatorio* and *Paradiso*. The most beautiful material is in the heavenly *Paradiso*. Dante's masterpiece is a narrative poem that is meant to teach. It is an allegory where the literal sense has a parallel, deeper symbolic sense. High art – like Dante's *Divine Comedy* – reveals truths. In the *Divine Comedy's* narrative, the pilgrim Dante travels down to the pit of Hell, then up Mount Purgatory and finally above to Heaven where God dwells. As an allegory, the pilgrim represents each of us here on earth and our journey to God. The goal of the story is to encourage the reader to seek God and be in His presence. Some of us here on earth may experience a bit of hell or may have to labor in purgatorial state, but our most beautiful experiences are when we are in the presence of God in the heavenly realm. The poem depicts God as an intense bright Light who is surrounded by nine rings of angels. This is significant because it comes from *The Celestial Hierarchy*. Dante, as a master teacher, applied to his art lessons from *The Celestial Hierarchy* – the focus of the present exposition. This simply shows the tremendous influence in both time and space that *The Celestial Hierarchy* has had in the world. In the poem, Dante describes the abode of God where there is a snow-white rose that represents divine love. It is the home for all the inhabitants of Heaven and there we discover angels flying around like bees distributing peace and love. Just as angels minister to those in Dante's poem *Paradiso*, so, too, do angels minister to those close to God in our world.

In our non-allegorical actual existence, angels, in most cases, are a part of the invisible community of the Church with the saints and God. In the Eastern Orthodox Church, on Sundays and holidays – when we are present in church and participate in the liturgical services – we pray, sing and give honor to those in Heaven. We ask them to intercede for us, so we, too, can join them and enjoy Heaven with them. As we worship in church, the invisible and visible come together as Heaven and earth are united during the liturgical services.

Are there evil angels? Yes, they are known as demons. Satan is the leader of the evil angels. Satan was an angel who fell from God because of his pride and self-centeredness, because of his excessive self-worth and self-worship. Satan rebelled against God looking to become his own god. Jesus is more powerful than Satan because Jesus is God's Son sharing God's Divinity, while Satan is merely a fallen creature. Demons are real. People often battle their demons as they struggle with sin but also with drug abuse, forms of addiction, depression and mental illness. We all struggle with and battle demons.

Saint Augustine says in his *The City of God* that the angels were created when God said, "Let there be light" (Genesis 1:3, RSV). All angels were created to be filled with God's Light and those who were loyal to God remained light; however, the angels who rejected God fell into darkness and are no longer filled with God's Light. God divided the light from the darkness as He distinguished the good from the evil.

Who are the two most famous angels? The two most famous angels are probably Archangels Michael and Gabriel. There are beautiful narratives of them in both the Old Testament and New Testament Scriptures.

Saint Michael the Archangel is referred to in the Old Testament's Book of Daniel at the prophecy of the resurrection of the dead. It is written, "At that time shall arise Michael, the great prince who has charge of your people" (Daniel 12:1, RSV). Archangel Michael is also referred to in the New Testament's Book of Revelation where it is prophesied that Michael and his army of angels defeats the Dragon Satan and his angels. In Revelation 12:7-12 (RSV), it is written,

> Now war arose in heaven, Michael and his angels fighting against the dragon; and the dragon and his angels fought, 8 but they were

defeated and there was no longer any place for them in heaven. 9 And the great dragon was thrown down, that ancient serpent, who is called the Devil and Satan, the deceiver of the whole world—he was thrown down to the earth, and his angels were thrown down with him. 10 And I heard a loud voice in heaven, saying, "Now the salvation and the power and the kingdom of our God and the authority of his Christ have come, for the accuser of our brethren has been thrown down, who accuses them day and night before our God. 11 And they have conquered him by the blood of the Lamb and by the word of their testimony, for they loved not their lives even unto death. 12 Rejoice then, O heaven and you that dwell therein! But woe to you, O earth and sea, for the devil has come down to you in great wrath, because he knows that his time is short!

Saint Michael the Archangel is always pictured with armor and a sword. He is a warrior. He is the leader of God's army against Satan.

Saint Gabriel the Archangel appears in the Old Testament's Book of Daniel to give the Prophet Daniel wisdom and understanding. Archangel Gabriel also appears in the New Testament to foretell Jesus's birth to the Virgin Mary. In Luke 1:26-38 (RSV), it is written,

In the sixth month the angel Gabriel was sent from God to a city of Galilee named Nazareth, 27 to a virgin betrothed to a man whose name was Joseph, of the house of David; and the virgin's name was Mary. 28 And he came to her and said, "Hail, O favored one, the Lord is with you!"[a] 29 But she was greatly troubled at the saying, and considered in her mind what sort of greeting this might be. 30 And the angel said to her, "Do not be afraid, Mary, for you have found favor with God. 31 And behold, you will conceive in your womb and bear a son, and you shall call his name Jesus. 32 He will be great, and will be called the Son of the Most High; and the Lord God will give to him the throne of his father David, 33 and he will reign over the house of Jacob for ever; and of his kingdom there will be no end." 34 And Mary said to the angel, "How shall this be, since I have no husband?" 35 And the angel said to her, "The Holy Spirit will come upon you, and the power of the Most High will overshadow you; therefore the child to be born[b] will be called holy, the Son of God. 36 And behold, your kinswoman Elizabeth in her old age has also conceived a son; and this is the sixth month with her who was called barren. 37 For with God nothing will be impossible." 38 And Mary said, "Behold, I am the handmaid of the Lord; let it be to me according to your word." And the angel departed from her.

Saint Gabriel the Archangel is often pictured with a horn or trumpet declaring good news from God or announcing the resurrection of the dead on Judgement Day.

In this exposition, we will investigate the heavenly realm of the holy angels by examining *The Celestial Hierarchy* written by a theologian identified as Dionysius the Areopagite. The author was a Christian from the 5th century AD, and he describes the community of nine types of angels in the celestial hierarchy. Celestial means heavenly. Hierarchy means ranking. By examining Scripture, Dionysius discovered the hierarchy or rank among the nine types of angels. Higher in the hierarchy – the closer to God and emitting blessings to those further from God. The closer to God, the more the angels take on God's qualities and minster to those below. Now, to be clear, Michael and Gabriel have very important roles in God's Divine Plan, but they are archangels, which is a type of angel in the lowest realm of the angelic ranks. *The Celestial Hierarchy* describes the organization of the angelic community. The celestial hierarchy is an order that human beings emulate in the Church and the National Armed Forces with each member working for a common cause or mission.

Some may ask, "Why is it important to know the hierarchy of celestial beings?" The purpose of the celestial hierarchy is to bring everyone closer to God according to each's capacity and merit, so they can reach theosis – the Greek term for deification and divinization (being made divine). This way we can all enjoy God's Light and Love in the heavenly realm. The text explains in Chapter III,

> The aim of Hierarchy is the greatest possible assimilation to and union with God, and by taking Him as leader in all holy wisdom, to become like Him, so far as is permitted, by contemplating intently His most Divine Beauty. Also it moulds and perfects its participants in the holy image of God like bright and spotless mirrors which receive the Ray of the Supreme Deity — which is the Source of Light; and being mystically filled with the Gift of Light, it pours it forth again abundantly, according to the Divine Law, upon those below itself. For it is not lawful for those who impart or participate in the holy Mysteries to overpass the bounds of its sacred laws; nor must they deviate from them if they seek to behold, as far as is allowed, that Deific Splendour and to be transformed into the likeness of those Divine Intelligences.
>
> Therefore he who speaks of Hierarchy implies a certain perfectly holy Order in the likeness of the First Divine Beauty, ministering the sacred mystery of its own

illuminations in hierarchical order and wisdom, being in due measure conformed to its own Principle.

For each of those who is allotted a place in the Divine Order finds his perfection in being uplifted, according to his capacity , towards the Divine Likeness; and what is still more divine, he becomes, as the Scriptures say, a fellow-worker with God, and shows forth the Divine Activity revealed as far as possible 'in himself. For the holy constitution of the Hierarchy ordains that some are purified, others purify; some are enlightened, others enlighten; some are perfected, others make perfect; for in this way the divine imitation will fit each one.

This exposition is a summary and analysis of the most influential and respected document on angels in Christendom. The masterpiece was formative in Eastern Christian theology, and it was influential in Western Christian theology through the works of giant figures like Saint Thomas Aquinas. The masterpiece is dense, intense and rich, but it may be difficult to follow for the uncommitted reader. The benefit of this exposition is that it is easier to read without losing the integrity of the theological lessons from the masterpiece.

The Celestial Hierarchy Analysis

Chapter I. To My Fellow-Presbyter Timothy, Dionysius the Presbyter

The masterpiece describes Celestial Beings as divine illuminations who go forth with love, remain one, unify and are constantly flowing to us. The source of the Angels' gifts is God – the Father of Lights. God is described as Father, Shepherding, Source of Divinity, Origin of Lights. The Light of the Father is Jesus – "The true light that enlightens every man was coming into the world" (John 1:9) who is the way to the Father (John 14:6). God – the Origin and Source of Everything – manifests, uplifts and governs His creatures in His universe. He elevates and unites with those who turn toward Him.

God has given us the Church, which imitates the Celestial Hierarchy and describes the Celestial in material terms, so that we might be led from holy imagery derived from things like sweet incense and candle lights to the formless. Receiving the most holy Eucharist symbolizes our participation with Jesus and everything else is given to us in symbols. God allows us to use symbols in the Church to understand Him and the Celestial realm. Furthermore, God describes the Celestial Hierarchy of Angels through figurative symbols in Scripture, so that we may be guided to Him for our deification because He loves us.

Chapter II. That Divine and Celestial Matters are Fittingly Revealed Even Through Unlike Symbols

Dionysius begins by breaking down his approach in leading us in the investigation of the Celestial Hierarchy. Firstly, we must examine the purpose of each Hierarchy and the goods bestowed upon followers. Secondly, we must celebrate the Hierarchies as they are revealed in Scripture. Finally, we must examine how the Celestial and Divine Intelligences are described in Scripture as many-footed, many-faced, brutish, and so on.

The descriptions of the Celestial Beings should not be taken literally but, rather, symbolically. In this regard, theology is designed to use poetic symbolism for our upliftment. However, some would prefer to regard the Divine Orders as pure, ineffable [indescribable], exalted and not in low earthly forms. Those who object to these extraordinary descriptions say it leads our minds into error.

The author Dionysius thinks that Scripture is perfect and neither dishonors the Divine Powers nor are we bound to earth by the baseness of the images. He provides two reasons that he thinks support his positive conclusion of base unlike symbols. He explains that our feeble intellect cannot contemplate the spiritual and, therefore, it needs encouragement from forms perceptible to us. In addition, these ineffable enigmas are not meant for the multitude and are reserved for the holy and knowledgeable.

The most holy Mysteries are set forth in two modes: similar akin to their nature and unlike forms with every possible discordance. The author provides examples for similar representations, such as when the Sublime Blessedness of the Superessential ONE is made equivalent to Light and Life. However, the mode of expression or articulation applied to our Transcendent God that is more appropriate is in negative theological terms rather than in positive terms (this is also known as the apophatic approach) because no description can fully represent God since He is Invisible (Not-Visible), Infinite (Not-Finite) and Unbound (Not-Bound). This mode of expression provides insight in the way we should read Scripture to imagine the mysterious nature of the transcendent Celestial Powers. The symbols are unlike the true nature of the Divine – the Ineffable. This mode of description by using unlike symbols is more appropriate for the Divinely Mysterious because this method honors rather than dishonors the Celestial because unlike images are far beyond all mundane things and uplift the mind more than the harmonious. Noble, golden, shining, glittering imagery describes visible beauty – which the Celestial is above. The ugliness of disharmony arouses the soul upward and stimulates it since no one would say such low forms resemble the Celestial. Moreover, nothing is deprived of beauty since all things are beautiful.

The meanings of words are different in the material realm from the intellectual realm. The material can symbolize the intellectual. And, words can have different meanings – for instance, passion in irrational creatures is desire, but passion in intellectual beings is unwavering steadfastness. When referring to Intellectual Celestial Beings, desire means divine love for the Immaterial, the purest Light, the perfect Beauty. When referring to the Celestial, incontinence [lack of self-restraint] means intense, unswerving, irresistible love of the Divine.

Another reason why it is lawful to portray Celestial Beings through the lowest material things is that even the lowest have vestiges [traces] of Intellectual Beauty. Theologians also use unlike poetic imagery to describe things other than the Celestial Orders – like when they describe God as the Sun of justice and Morning Star of the mind. Other types of lowest images that are also used by theologians include fragrant ointment, cornerstone, lion, bear, worm. Why do theologians prefer to use incongruous symbols? They do this so divine things may not be easily accessible to the unworthy and so people do not dwell upon the forms as the final truth. The benefit and intent of using discordant symbols for the Celestial Natures is that the descriptions prompt us to search into the Mysteries which lead us to the Heights. The ugliness of the imagery of the Celestial

Beings startles us and stimulates us to leave behind all material attachments for the super mundane [supernatural] ascent.

Chapter III. What is Hierarchy, and What the Use of Hierarchy?

According to Dionysius, Hierarchy is a holy order which participates in the Divine Likeness. God bestows his gifts to the creatures of His Creation according to each's merit. The aim of the Hierarchy is assimilation to and union with God. This is beautifully expressed in the masterpiece,

> The aim of Hierarchy is the greatest possible assimilation to and union with God, and by taking Him as leader in all holy wisdom, to become like Him, so far as is permitted, by contemplating intently His most Divine Beauty. Also it moulds and perfects its participants in the holy image of God like bright and spotless mirrors which receive the Ray of the Supreme Deity — which is the Source of Light; and being mystically filled with the Gift of Light, it pours it forth again abundantly, according to the Divine Law, upon those below itself. For it is not lawful for those who impart or participate in the holy Mysteries to overpass the bounds of its sacred

laws; nor must they deviate from them if they seek to behold, as far as is allowed, that Deific Splendour and to be transformed into the likeness of those Divine Intelligences.

Those who are allotted a place in the Divine Order are uplifted, according to their capacities, towards Divine Likeness to become fellow workers with God in Divine Activity. Dionysius describes how this leads to Divine Bliss. He explains, "Inasmuch as the Divine Bliss (to speak in human terms) is exempt from all dissimilarity, and is full of Eternal Light, perfect, in need of no perfection, purifying, illuminating, perfecting being rather Himself the holy Purification, Illumination and Perfection, above purification, above light. supremely perfect, Himself the origin of perfection and the cause of every Hierarchy, He transcends in excellence all holiness." Here, Dionysius illustrates what it is like to participate with God and how that leads to Divine Bliss.

The phases in the Hierarchical structure include purification, illumination and initiation. What should those who are active in those phases be doing for others? Those who purify should bestow their holiness. Those who illuminate should impart their light. Those who initiate should lead others to perfection. Humankind can learn from this. Humankind should imitate the God loving Celestial Intelligences' divine cooperation.

Chapter IV. The Meaning of the Name 'Angels'.

We should treat the Angelic Hierarchy with honor so that we may be uplifted to their divine purity and may praise God. From each creature God created, God expects each to participate in God in proportion to the capacity and nature of each. In God's universe there exist inanimate things, living things, and rational things. Angels surpass in participation other things in God's universe by molding themselves intelligibly to the imitation of God; they have more abundant communion with Him with never relaxing activity up the ascent through unwearying divine love in a life wholly intellectual.

Angels have been in historical contact with our forefathers: angels gave us the Law; angels guided our illustrious forefathers on what they should do, away from error to the straight path of truth; angels showed them the Holy Hierarchies, secret visions, and divine prophecies.

Dionysius makes clear that no human being has ever seen God Almighty. However, God shows Himself to His faithful servants through holy visions adapted to the nature of the seer. The theological term for the visible manifestation of God to humankind is theophany. Dionysius explains that it is the Celestial Powers known as Angels who mediate between God and humankind. Angels communicate to each other through the ranks – the higher are initiators and guides of the lower. Some New Testament examples the author gives of an Angel mediating between God and humankind include when Gabriel announced to John the Baptist's father Zachariah of his son's birth, and when Gabriel revealed to the Virgin Mary that she would give birth to the ineffable Incarnation of God. Another Angel spoke to Joseph, and another to the shepherds.

The Head of the Supercelestial Beings is Jesus. Another angelic title of Jesus is "Angel of Good Counsel." He is given this title because whatsoever He heard from the Father, He announced unto us.

Chapter V. Why All the Celestial Beings in Common are Called Angels.

Theologians give the name Angel to all Celestial Beings. In the Celestial Hierarchy, the name Angel specifies a Celestial Being at the lowest rank. The Celestial Beings called Angels complete and conclude the Divine Celestial Hierarchy. The reason why all Celestial Beings from the highest to the lowest are given the name Angel is because the highest orders possess the illuminations and powers of the lower ranks with the lowest known as Angels. The lower do not participate equally with those above them, so it would be incorrect to call the lowest

Seraphim (the name of the highest Celestial Beings). All can be rightly called Angels because all participate in that Divine Likeness. Regarding the relationship between the higher and the lower of the Celestial Beings, the higher possess in full the strengths of the lower, but the lower do not possess in full the strengths of the higher.

Chapter VI. Which is the First Order of the Celestial Beings, Which the Middle, and Which the Last?

In identifying the known Celestial Beings, theology has assigned them nine interpretive names. In the Celestial Hierarchy, there are three threefold Orders. First are the Seraphim, Cherubim and Thrones. They dwell eternally in God's constant presence. They cleave to Him, are united to Him and are nearest to Him above all others. This threefold Order has a co-equal unity and are the most exalted and the most fully Godlike. Second are the Dominions, Virtues and Powers. Last and lowest are the Principalities, Archangels and Angels. The names were given to each Celestial Intelligence according to each's Archetype [Essence] in God with a name corresponding to the property in God which it exhibits. All these Celestial Beings, in a common fashion, receive from above and deliver below. They are constantly receiving, informing, purifying, enlightening, perfecting and representing the Divine Truth and Light.

Chapter VII. Of the Seraphim, Cherubim and Thrones, and Their First Hierarchy.

The names of the Celestial Beings in the first (and highest) Hierarchy are Seraphim, Cherubim, and Thrones. There is oneness among them in that they are co-equal, yet there is also diversity among them in that they imitate God as far as their nature permits.

In Hebrew, Seraphim means those who kindle or make hot. This is an appropriate name for them because it indicates their ceaseless and eternal revolution about Divine Principles and their heat, keenness and perpetual activity as they purify those below – destroying the shadows of darkness. They burn brightly with the Eternal Love of God. Since God is Agape Love (1 John 4:8b) and the Seraphim are nearest of all creatures to the Creator and most passionately imitate Him, the Seraphim embody agape love. They "may be called wise Loves" (VI, footnote, ccel.org). There are saints and monks who have been baptized with the name Seraphim.

Of the Cherubim, their name denotes their knowing and beholding God, their contemplating the Beauty of the Godhead in Its First Manifestation. They are filled with, participate in and embody Divine Wisdom. They "may be called loving

Wisdoms" (VI, footnote, ccel.org). And, they outpour wisdom to those below. The name Cherub has been adopted by popular culture and is used to identify the angelic winged babies who decorate cards for Valentine's Day. This image has nothing in common with the art of traditional angelology where a Cherub is a lion or bull with eagles' wings and a human face.

Of the Thrones, their name denotes how they are untainted by base and earthly things. They ascent up the steep and have no part in that which is lowest. They are above all passion and matter. They, too, are loving and wise, but they primarily embody God's Firmness and Justice.

"Thus does God beam forth with firmness, wisdom and love in the Thrones, Cherubs and Seraphs" (VI, footnote, ccel.org). The goal, objective and purpose of the Hierarchy is steadfast devotion to divine assimilation in the Likeness of God. "Among them all, in every threefold manner, there is a striving with all their might to imitate God" (VI, footnote, ccel.org).

Those First Beings – who are established after the Godhead – are understood to be pure. In the masterpiece, as learned from Scripture, Dionysius explains,

> … they are pure, not as having been cleansed from stains and defilements, nor as not admitting material images, but as far higher

than all baseness, and surpassing all that is holy. As befits the highest purity, they are established above the most Godlike Powers and eternally keep their own self-motive and self-same order through the Eternal Love of God, never weakening in power, abiding most purely in their own Godlike identity, ever unshaken and unchanging. Again, they are contemplative, not as beholding intellectual or sensible symbols, nor as being uplifted to the Divine by the all-various contemplations set forth in the Scriptures, but as filled with Light higher than all immaterial knowledge, and rapt, as is meet, in the contemplation of that Beauty which is the superessential triune Origin and Creator of all beauty. In like manner they are thought worthy of fellowship with Jesus, not through sacred images which shadow forth the Divine Likeness, but as truly being close to Him in that first participation of the knowledge of His Deifying Illuminations. Moreover, the imitation of God is granted to them in a preeminent degree, and as far as their nature permits, they share the divine and human virtues in primary power.

They are also perfect. Dionysius explains,

> In the same manner they are perfect, not as though enlightened by an analytical

knowledge of holy variety, but because they are wholly perfected through the highest and most perfect deification, possessing the highest knowledge that Angels can have of the works of God; being Hierarchs not through other holy beings, but from God Himself, and since they are uplifted to God directly by their pre-eminent power and rank, they are both established immovably beside the All-Holy, and are borne up, as far as is allowable, to the contemplation of His Intelligible and Spiritual Beauty. Being placed nearest to God, they are instructed in the true understanding of the divine works, and receive their hierarchical order in the highest degree from Deity Itself, the First Principle of Perfection.

The lower ranks receive divine understanding from those above them. One may wonder if Angels can ask Jesus questions and Dionysius positively affirms this. Why do Angels ask Jesus questions? They do so to obtain knowledge for us. Jesus is depicted as teaching them. Those in the first rank first go about receiving divine enlightenment in an intermediate manner by first questioning one another without expectation of the enlightenment divinely granted to them. The first Hierarchy is not tainted by any inferiority. The following is what existence is like for the first Order,

This, so far as I know, is the first Order of Celestial Beings which are established about God, immediately encircling Him: and in perpetual purity they encompass His eternal Knowledge in that most high and eternal angelic dance, rapt in the bliss of manifold blessed contemplations, and irradiated with pure and primal splendours.

The are filled with divine food which is manifold, through the first-given outpouring, yet one through the unvaried and unific oneness of the divine banquet; and they are deemed worthy of communion and co-operation with God by reason of their assimilation to Him, as far as is possible for them, in the excellence of their natures and energies. For they know pre-eminently many divine matters, and they participate as far as they may in Divine Understanding and Knowledge.

That Hierarchy sings hymns as a choir. Dionysius explains,

> Wherefore theology has given those on earth its hymns or praise in which is divinely shown forth the great excellence of its sublime illumination. For some of that choir (to use material terms) cry out as with a voice like the sound of many waters, 'Blessed is the Glory

of the Lord from His Place'; others cry aloud that most renowned and sacred hymn of highest praise to God, 'Holy, holy, holy, Lord God of Sabaoth, the whole earth is full of Thy Glory!'

They only cry out to Glorify God. The first Order teaches all below to give God the Glory that He is due. God is the super-original Principle and Cause of every essence and holds the whole universe superessentially in His irresistible embrace.

Chapter VIII. Of the Dominions, Virtues and Powers, and Their Middle Hierarchy.

The names of the Celestial Beings in the middle Hierarchy are Dominions, Virtues and Powers.

The name Dominions signifies unbound elevation to that which is above and freedom from all that is of the earth. They are exempt from the low. They possess lordship. They fashion themselves and those below with true lordship.

The name Virtues signifies powerful and unshakable virility. They possess stronghold. They are not weak or feeble. They fashion themselves and those below in virtue.

The name Powers signifies orderly and unconfined order. They possess authority. They beneficently lead those below them to the Supreme Power.

Those in the middle rank have relationships to the Celestial Intelligences who are above and those who are below. They are purified, illuminated and perfected in a secondary manner through the first hierarchical Order and shine forth in a secondary manifestation to those who are below them. Knowledge and Light are affected when they reach the second rank and then, in turn, to those below. Knowledge and Light are from above and made obscure through the ranks, which act as intermediaries. The Divine Light's direct revelations impart a greater perfection. The Order of Angels nearest to the Godhead participates in a more resplendent light than is imparted to those who are perfected through others.

Then, Dionysius references Prophet Zachariah's testimony regarding angels. He continues by referencing Prophet Ezekiel's testimony regarding angels which can be found in the Old Testament's Book of Ezekiel and is known as "The Slaughter of the Idolaters". It is a powerful example of Angelic orders in action doing God's work. Then, Dionysius references Prophet Daniel's testimony regarding angels. Daniel had visions, which were explained to him by Archangel Gabriel.

Why does knowing about the Celestial Hierarchy matter? We should apply that knowledge to our hierarchy to help us. By molding itself after the angelic likeness, our own hierarchy will be assimilated to it and will show forth angelic beauty and be uplifted by the Celestial Hierarchy.

Chapter IX. Of the Principalities, Archangels and Angels, and Of Their Last Hierarchy.

The names of the Celestial Beings in the last (and lowest) Hierarchy are Principalities, Archangels and Angels.

The name Principalities signifies their Godlike princeliness and authoritativeness as they are wholly turned towards the Prince of Princes and lead others in princely fashion. They rule and protect.

Next are the Archangels. There is a unique relationship between the Archangels and the other two ranks of this final Hierarchy. Archangels are in the middle, but they participate in the two extremes of this threefold Hierarchy. They are turned in a princely way to the Superessential Principalities and are joined with the Angels in the interpreting Order by receiving from the First Powers and announcing to the Angels below. Archangels are chief messengers.

The name Angels identifies the final rank in the Hierarchy. They complete the lowest choir of all the Hierarchies and are the last of the angelic natures. Angels receive announcements from Archangels and show revelations to us human beings in the manifested and mundane domain. Angels are messengers.

The Celestial Hierarchy has a structured system and organization that reaches down to the human hierarchies. The highest Order is nearest to God above the second Order, which in turn leads the lower more manifestly than the higher. The Hierarchy of Principalities, Archangels and Angels presides over the human hierarchies, so their elevation and turning to God and their communion and union with Him may be in order. The Hierarchy and organization of Angels is seen in the Church and the National Armed Forces. Members receive from above and deliver to those below. Nothing skips a level. Each level has a place. The hierarchies are organized and work for a common cause or mission.

Angels have a unique role on people and the nations. The Word of God has given our human hierarchy into the care of Angels and has assigned an Angel to each nation. Some may ask, "If Angels have been assigned to all nations, why have only the Jews been guided to the Divine?" This is because the other nations turned away to false gods, not by the direct guidance of their Angels but because of their refusal of the true path and their self-love and perversity. Unfortunately, the Jews have also fallen into error because of their own heart and unacceptance and resistance to God. Some may ask, "Then, who can be saved?" Dionysius explains that those who listen to God and His Angels will be saved. We must listen to

God the Father and His Son and the Holy Spirit in Tri-Unity.

Dionysius points out the example of the saved and cherished Priest-King Melchizedek, who was a leader of others in the ascent to God. Dionysius points out examples of Angels presiding over the nations of Egypt, Babylon and Israel. The examples show us that God has assigned Angels to all Nations, but only the Israelites listened to God and their Angels. Which Angel was the leader of the Jewish Nation? Michael.

Chapter X. Recapitulation and Summary of the Angelic Hierarchies.

The Hierarchical system reaches us when the Highest Most Venerable Hierarchy is purified, illuminated and perfected by the Light of the Godhead and then when the second Hierarchy is, as well, in its own degree, and by the second the third, and by the third our hierarchy.

It is important that the Hierarchy be organized because each Order is the interpreter of those above it – the most venerable being the interpreter of God. The establishment of the beautiful choirs of each Hierarchy – with each Hierarchy possessing first, middle and last powers – has provided the superessential harmony of all things.

This knowledge of the Hierarchy pertains to each of us because each Celestial and human intelligence contains within itself its own first, middle and last powers analogous to the Hierarchical illuminations (In a similar manner, ancient Greek philosopher Plato explained – in his *The Republic* – the hierarchy within the soul). Plus, each of us, as intelligent beings, can participate – like the Celestial Beings do – in the most complete perfection with God.

Chapter XI. Why All the Celestial Hierarchies in Common are called Celestial Powers.

The general name Celestial Powers identifies all the Holy Angelic Beings. The term Celestial Powers is meant to be used to properly include all Divine Intelligences from highest to lowest in common indirectly with respect to each's power. However, we should not assign the characteristics of the highest rank of Holy Powers to the Celestial Beings below them because the lowest do not fully possess the principles of those more venerable than themselves – even though the highest Orders fully possess the holy characteristics of the lower.

Chapter XII. Why the Hierarchs Among Men are Called Angels.

The Cherubim participate in high wisdom and those below them partake in that wisdom to the degree of and in proportion to their capacity. In accordance with each one's rank, the lowest possesses the powers of the higher, not in equal measure, but to a subordinate degree. Using this logic, it is not inappropriate to call a human hierarch by the name Angel because of one's participation – according to one's own power – in the interpretive characteristic of the Angels and assimilation to the Angels as revealers of truth. This is similar to when Celestial Beings or even saintly men are called gods because even though it is clear that neither is in fact God or even close to being like God, they do share qualities with God. They are partakers in God's Divinity and on occasion are assigned the name gods.

Chapter XIII. The Reason Why the Prophet Isaiah is Said to Have Been Purified by the Seraphim.

Of all the theology in the masterpiece, the ideas in this section are the most inconclusive – as the author himself admits at the end. It is the most speculative and difficult to follow. Even so, there are great truths and analogies revealed here.

This section is about the Prophet Isaiah and his encounter with and being purified by one of the Seraphim. This is unique because a Seraph is in the highest rank and the cleansing of a prophet (a human being) is the work of a lower rank Angel. Due to the interrelations of the Celestial Intelligences, some explain this by suggesting that the Angel was not of the highest rank but a Guardian Angel who was given the sacred function of purifying the prophet through fire which is the work of the Seraphim and therefore the Angel was given the name of Seraph. An alternative solution to the way in which one of the Seraphim could have purified the prophet Isaiah is that the great Angel, who fashioned the vision for the prophet, appealed to God and after God, to that first hierarchy which descended to the lower hierarchies and then finally to the prophet Isaiah. This is possible since that Divine First Power penetrates all things invisibly in a hidden way.

    The author Dionysius provides two examples from the natural material order to illustrate the way God transmits His Energies. Example one is the light of the sun which passes readily through transparent first matter, then through denser material less brightly, until it hardly passes through at all. Similarly, example two is the heat of fire which first heats material that is easily made hot and through it, to other substances that do not so easily become hot. These natural material examples are analogous to the way God transmits His Energies in the Celestial and human hierarchies. Those in the highest rank are given the highest knowledge because they desire it the most and are thought worthy to become first workers of the imitation of God. In the hierarchies from highest to lowest, all participate in the measure of their receptivity. The lower Celestial ranks receive the level of knowledge they do because it is given according to their receptivity and openness to God.

Returning to the Prophet Isaiah and the Seraphim, an alternate explanation suggests that a holy Angel, who presides over us, raised – through his enlightening guidance – the Prophet Isaiah to the intellectual contemplation of the Seraphim who are around God Who is above all.

From the visions, the prophet learned about God and the Celestial Hierarchy. He learned that God is the source of everything and that He cares for and energizes everything below Him.

Then, the prophet was instructed that the Seraphim – "The Fiery Ones" – led the upliftment towards the Divine Likeness. The Seraphim are physically described as having sixfold wings as well as many feet and many faces where the eyes and feet are covered by wings and their middle wings are in ceaseless movement. Through the vision, the prophet Isaiah learned about the Seraphim. He learned about their farreaching and farseeing powers, their holy awe and search into higher and deeper Mysteries, their ceaseless activity in imitation of God as they soar to the heights. Dionysius points out how the prophet also learned that "divine and most glorious song of praise" which is found in the Book of Isaiah 6:1-8 where the Seraphim fly around the Throne of God crying "holy, holy, holy" – a formula that came to be known as the Trisagion (Thrice-Holy) prayer.

Participation in the Divine purifies the participant as shown most clearly and fully in the exalted Powers around God. The Divine Ray (or Energy) originates in the Uncreated who is Unmanifested and manifests through the Celestial Hierarchy. Purification is imparted in measure of the fitness of each for the divine participations.

Returning to the original question, it is reasonable to say a Seraph purified Prophet Isaiah in the same way that God Himself purifies all below Him. Similarly, a human hierarch, through his priests, consecrates sacred activity. And, therefore, it is possible that the Angel who purified the prophet could have attributed the performance – after God – to the Seraph who taught him and who thereby is responsible – after God – for the purification.

Are the conclusions in this section that the author sets forth perfect? Are his views in this section definitive? Dionysius confesses that it is up to a person's intellectual and discriminating skills to accept these solutions as probable or reasonable. Otherwise, it is up to a person to find from oneself something more true or from another, a clearer view.

The author ends this section by leaving it open ended for us to decide – which is very humble and honest. Because the author appears honest, this section gives his other sections greater credibility when he is more definitive, conclusive, forceful and sure. Honesty takes an author and teacher a long way when leading his audience.

Chapter XIV. What the Traditional Number of the Angels Signifies.

The traditional number of the Angels is numbered as thousands of thousands and ten thousand times ten thousand. This signifies that the Celestial Beings are innumerable to us – surpassing the feeble and limited range of our material numbers.

Chapter XV. What is the Meaning of the Formal Semblances of the Angelic Powers?

Celestial Beings are described with unique designated formal semblances, such as with fiery and anthropomorphic qualities. They are described with ears, wings, shining raiment, battle-axes and described as clouds, brass, choirs, jewels, lions, horses, chariots. These descriptions of the Celestial Beings are meant to be taken symbolically. They are also described as possessing Angelic joy.

As the Celestial Beings are led by those above and lead those below, Scripture sometimes uses sacred symbolism that assigns the same powers to the first, middle and last ranks. All Celestial Beings eagerly tend upward to those above and participate with those below – some pre-eminently, others to a lower degree.

Of all the symbols in Scripture, the highest preference is given to fire – with descriptions like fiery wheels, lightening, rivers of flame. And, we find that fire is the most preferred symbol to describe the Celestial Beings. The author Dionysius thinks all this mention of fire signifies the perfect conformity of the Celestial Intelligences to God. Fire resembles best the Divine Reality and Divine activity. Dionysius explains,

> Therefore I think that this image of fire signifies the perfect conformity to God of the Celestial Intelligences For the holy prophets frequently liken that which is superessential and formless to fire which (if it may lawfully be said) possesses many resemblances as in visible things to the Divine Reality. For the sensible fire is in some manner in everything, and pervades all things without mingling with them, and is exempt from all things and, although wholly bright, yet lies essentially hidden and unknown when not in contact with any substance on which it can exert its own energy. It is irresistible and invisible, having absolute rule over all things, bringing under its own power all things in which it subsists. It has transforming power, and imparts itself in some measure to everything near it. It revives

all things by its revivifying heat, and illuminates them all with its resplendent brightness. It is insuperable and pure, possessing separative power, but itself changeless, uplifting, penetrative, high, not held back by servile baseness, ever-moving, selfmoved, moving other things. It comprehends, but is incomprehensible, unindigent, mysteriously increasing itself and showing forth its majesty according to the nature of the substance receiving it, powerful, mighty, invisibly present to all things. When not thought of, it seems not to exist, but suddenly enkindles its light in the way proper to its nature by friction, as though seeking to do so, uncontrollably flying upwards without diminishing its all-blessed self-giving.

Knowing this, we see how Celestial Beings are portrayed under the figure of fire to proclaim their likeness to the Divine and their imitation of Him.

Celestial Beings are given the likeness not only of fire but also of humankind. This is because of the human powers of intellect and aspiration, the powers of guiding and governing as well as because man rules over creatures. In addition, man possesses the lordship of rational knowledge and the intrinsic freedom of his unconquerable soul.

The first physical characteristic of man that the author mentions that applies to Celestial Beings is sight and this is appropriate because of sight's upliftment to and reception of the Divine Light and divine illuminations. Other sensory powers of man that are equated to the Celestial Beings include the ability to smell, hear, taste, touch. Dionysius proceeds to explain why in the masterpiece. Other human body parts that are associated to Celestial Beings are eyelids and eyebrows, teeth, shoulders, arms, hands, heart, chest, back, feet as well as youth and vigor. Dionysius proceeds to explain why in the masterpiece.

Two other separate categories used to describe Celestial Beings are garments and instruments. The two types of garments are shining/fiery and priestly. In the masterpiece, we learn why they are used. Three instrument types that the author points out are rods, spears/battle-axes and carpenters' tools. In the masterpiece, we learn why they are used. These visible symbols correspond to invisible realities.

Two powers from the natural earth that are applied to Celestial Beings are winds and clouds. Winds possess energy and force and are swift and mysterious. Clouds are filled with hidden Light and transmit it as well as shower fertilizing rains for life-giving travail. Celestial Beings are likened to natural substances and elements like brass/electron and colored jewels. Dionysius explains their mystical interpretation.

Four beasts or animals that resemble the Celestial Beings are the lion, ox, eagle and horse.

The text explains what we can learn about the Celestial Beings from the symbolism of these animals. Certain characteristics of animals are used to teach us about the Celestial Intelligences through dissimilar similitudes. Rivers, chariots and wheels are used as symbols in the visions of Celestial Beings.

The Celestial Beings are said to be filled with joy above and beyond our passionate pleasures. They rejoice with God at the finding of the lost. They are filled with boundless joy at the Salvation of those who are turned to God. And, they are filled with ineffable bliss in God's Illuminations.

The author confesses that this section is short of complete and short of full interpretation of the sacred symbols. Nonetheless, it is sufficient to prevent us from dwelling on the base figures themselves. He explains that some knowledge in Scripture regarding Angels is not ascertainable, or, perhaps, another guide will emerge to teach us more. He explains other things he has passed over but are parallel to what he has revealed. Finally, he says that the hidden Mysteries which lie beyond his view he has honored by silence.

Conclusion

The Celestial Hierarchy is a sincere, deep and authoritative analysis on the nature of Angels. The masterpiece is extremely influential in Eastern Christianity and has reached giant figures in Western Christianity such as Saint Thomas Aquinas and Dante Alighieri. As I pointed out in the introduction and as illustrated in the exposition, the goal from applying the principles taught in *The Celestial Hierarchy* is for the student to attain theosis – the Greek term for deification and divinization (being made divine). This is the aim of life as articulated in Christianity – particularly the Eastern Church – and is the clearest sign of Salvation. If we want to attain union with God and be filled with God-like qualities, we must emulate Him. *The Celestial Hierarchy* identifies God's most defining archetypes (essences) through the nine different Celestial Beings – commonly referred to as Angels. If a person desires theosis/deification/divinization, the person should embody God's Agape Love like the Seraphim, embody God's Wisdom like the Cherubim, embody God's Justice like the Thrones. The person should possess God's Lordship like the Dominions, possess God's Virtue and Stronghold like the Virtues, possess God's Authority like the Powers. The person should rule and protect as God does like the Principalities, be God's chief messenger like the Archangels, be God's messenger like the Angels. In addition, the person should imitate the Celestial Beings' organized discipline and their divine cooperation. These form the angelic method to theosis. Dionysius wrote his masterpiece to inspire us to attain theosis and if a person is inspired, the next step is to emulate to make the vision a reality. Amen.

Work Cited

- Dionysius the Areopagite. *The Celestial Hierarchy*. Christian Classics Ethereal Library: https://www.ccel.org. Accessed 11-23-2018.

MASTERPIECE: Saint Athanasius's *Life of Antony*

TITLE OF EXPOSITION: Saint Antony and the Way to Theosis

Description

The biography of a saint by a fellow saint, the *Life of Antony* by Athanasius is a masterpiece and a beautiful blend of story and lesson. Through Antony's life, Athanasius teaches his audience about asceticism (discipline), adversity (suffering), theosis (divinization) and Christian apologetics (defending Christianity). These are fundamental themes in Christianity, particularly Eastern Orthodox Christianity. The purpose of my exposition is not to critique Athanasius's *Life of Antony*; rather, I reorganize and analyze the literature to highlight the above-mentioned themes, so my readers can more clearly see, identify and understand them. I believe this will be particularly valuable for a person new to or still trying to grasp those themes. This is the type of material that helps me through life and may help you, as well. Enjoy and may God bless you.

Contents

First Half
+ Introduction
+ Asceticism
+ Adversity
  + Chrysostom on Adversity
+ More on Asceticism Against the Devil

Second Half
+ Theosis
+ Christian Apologetics
+ Antony's Death
+ More Theology on Theosis
  + Irenaeus on Theosis
  + Further Theology on Theosis
+ Conclusion
+ Bibliography and Works Cited

First Half

Introduction

The *Life of Antony's* author is Athanasius (c.295-373) – a saint who attended the first ecumenical council held in Nicaea in 325 where the Christian Creed began to take form. He became bishop of Alexandria, acquired the designation the Great and is known as the Father of Orthodox Christianity.

The *Life of Antony* is Athanasius's most influential writing. It was a literary sensation that quickly earned the status of a classic. It is a biography of the heroic, larger than life and revolutionary Egyptian desert monk Antony (c.251-356) – a fellow saint who, too, acquired the designation the Great and is considered the Father of Monasticism.

The literary form is adopted from classical literature about the lives of pagan heroes, and it inaugurated and became a model for Christian hagiography, which is the genre about the saints' lives. Antony's experiences identified features of Christian Salvation and sainthood that established patterns of experience for later saints. Antony was raised a Christian. He was not a convert, but he elevated what it means to be a Christian with his saintly life. He adhered to the Christian spiritual life as well as the ascetic tradition. What is asceticism? Asceticism is exercise or training for spiritual purification. It is about austere and rigorous discipline. Sometimes harsh and dramatic, other times moderate and learned, ascetic practice qualified the ideal devout life for the Church's members. Antony's life was a new kind of martyrdom. It is a martyrdom from the world and of the conscience where, through ascetic piety, one is reborn and rises into a new spiritual state and life.

Spiritual warfare against Satan and his forces was a continuous struggle for Antony, and it stands out in the text about his life – as does divine empowerment and God's grace. Demons are disturbers of the peace, but as shown in the text, Antony had mastery over Satan and his demons through his allegiance to Christ. Monks may retire from the world, but they face significant challenges and dangers. Life is hard for everyone – including those Christian monastics who have left the world's madness as well as all saints of all lifestyles – but Antony showed us that we all can defeat the devil and his demons through Jesus Christ.

Interestingly, even though Antony left society, he was still involved with people as they followed him into the desert. He was a source of answers and a worker of wonders. He was advanced in holiness, but there was great simplicity in his knowledge. He did not have a classical education, but he was spiritually wise.

His disciplined ascetic life brought about heavenly powers that were not his own. Antony's victories over demons were not attributed to his own powers – as he himself confessed. They were the works of Christ. Help and deliverance were derived only from Christ's divine power. Antony showed us that to attain any success, we are entirely dependent on Jesus who is our Savior and God. Greatness and victory against Satan and evil is only possible by being devoted to Jesus the Christ. We become deified and divinized (made divine) through Jesus the Christ. In Eastern Orthodox Christianity, this is known as theosis. This is Salvation through Jesus. As Church Father Saint Irenaeus said, God had "become what we are, that He might bring us to be even what He is Himself" (*Against Heresies: Book V*, "Preface," ccel.org).

Part of Antony's theosis – through God's grace and Jesus Christ – was his ability to defend the Christian Faith with apologetic teachings against pagan philosophy and heresy. By remaining in this orthodox tradition and teaching this orthodox theology – through writing the story of Antony's life – Athanasius fought heresy, particularly Arianism.

Antony pursued God in isolation, and it fascinated those still in society. His goals of individual perfection and holy living attracted many to Christianity. It was a bloodless martyrdom that helped the Church to flourish and helped to propagate the Faith. Through the *Life of Antony*, we can learn about ancient Christian spirituality and apply it to our modern lives for the growth and betterment of our minds and souls.

There is little that needs to be added to Athanasius's *Life of Antony* to improve it. It is a masterpiece and a beautiful blend of story and lesson. Through Antony's life, Athanasius teaches his audience about asceticism, adversity, theosis and Christian apologetics. These are fundamental themes in Christianity, particularly Eastern Orthodox Christianity. As a whole, the literature is articulate, inspiring and edifying. The purpose of my exposition is not to critique Athanasius's *Life of Antony*; rather, I will reorganize the literature to highlight the above-mentioned themes, so my readers can more clearly see, identify and understand them. I believe this will be particularly valuable for a person new to or still trying to grasp those themes. This exposition does not replace the masterpiece, which celebrates Antony's life. I encourage everyone to read the original. Antony is an extraordinary character, man and saint. However, I will systematically analyze and reorganize the work about his life to make the fundamental themes easier to grasp. My goal is to introduce and teach about asceticism, adversity, theosis and Christian apologetics, so my readers can apply the lessons to their own lives. The masterpiece is organized into 94 sections. As I highlight sections, I will identify them in parentheses.

Asceticism

Athanasius initially wrote the narrative for monks to inspire them to imitate Antony and his ascetic practice – which, as I said, is exercise or training for spiritual purification. There are many quotes from Scripture which give the work authenticity, relevance and authority.

The work was crafted in the form of a biography and so, in the beginning, we briefly learn about Antony's childhood (1). We also learn about his parents' deaths when he was about 20 years old and how he heard his calling. After his parents died, Antony sold his possessions and gave to the poor to follow the Lord – just as Jesus said: "If you would be perfect, go, sell what you possess and give to the poor, and you will have treasure in heaven; and come, follow me" (Matthew 19:21, RSV). Antony heard the Gospel message in church and took it as a sign from God – as if by God's design, the passage was read for him. What should we make of this? Is it normal? Is it crazy? Is it awesome? What does the author want us to see in the person of Antony? We come to realize that Antony was a faithful and extraordinary servant of the Lord (2).

Antony gave his sister into the care of trusted virgins at the convent, and then he began to walk on the road to virtue. The author talks about "the discipline," which is him referring to the ascetic lifestyle. Antony began learning the discipline in an effective way by emulating an old man in the solitary life. At this time, Antony was growing and becoming a man and making serious decisions about his life. He was praying and being attentive to Scripture. Memory took the place of books (3). He was living the discipline and gained recognition. Each of the ascetics Antony learned from taught him something different, and he was attentive to each's unique strengths. However, they were all alike in piety toward Christ and mutual love. Antony learned from each of them and emulated what was best from all (4).

Asceticism Continued

Then, adversity struck. The devil tried to stop Antony with worries. Even so, Antony persevered (7). He overcame the devil. After this victory through Christ, Antony did not get careless or arrogant, and the devil did not stop setting traps. The devil continued. (Antony's adversity with the devil and demons will be thoroughly reviewed in the next section.)

Antony's life was unique as were his physical living arrangements. He was watchful without sleep, ate bread and salt once daily and only drank water. He slept on a rush mat or the bare ground. Most people could not live such an austere, strict and simple lifestyle – to live without excess, comforts or indulgence. Antony lived by a great quote. He said, "the fibre of the soul is then sound when the pleasures of the body are diminished" (7, Schaff, ccel.org). Antony lived each day as a new beginning and was always prepared to obey God's will and was always ready to appear before God with a pure heart (7).

Asceticism Continued Further

After 20 years of asceticism, Antony's body and soul were clean. People began to emulate him and follow him into the desert (14). Antony's lifestyle was extreme, but some must have found this lifestyle noble. Certainly, some were fascinated, others curious, and still others inspired. 20 years is a long time to be living alone in the desert. Some readers may question if his body truly maintained its former condition. However, I can attest from visiting Orthodox Christian monasteries like Saint Nektarios Monastery in Roscoe, NY and the New Skete monastic community in Mount Athos, Greece that present day monastics retain healthy bodies and souls. We should not doubt that the state of Antony's soul was one of purity. As the text explains,

> And again his soul was free from blemish, for it was neither contracted as if by grief, nor relaxed by pleasure, nor possessed by laughter or dejection, for he was not troubled when he beheld the crowd, nor overjoyed at being saluted by so many. But he was altogether

even as being guided by reason, and abiding in a natural state" (14, Schaff, ccel.org).

Through Antony, God worked many blessings. He healed people physically, purged people from demons, consoled and reconciled people and gave Antony grace in speech. Because of Antony, the desert was transformed. The desert was made a city by monks (14). Many monasteries emerged, and Antony became like a father to all. He was also blessed with extraordinary powers, like when he prayed away crocodiles. Can we truly believe that crocodiles left Antony unharmed because of his prayers? It is not unlikely with the power of God and the calmness of His saints. We can even look at the popular Catholic Saint Francis of Assisi and his healthy and extraordinary relationship with nature. The above include some of the first signs of Antony's theosis or the power of God that was displayed in him (15). (Antony's theosis will be thoroughly reviewed later in the exposition.)

In sections 16-43, Athanasius wrote about Antony's discourse around the themes of asceticism and adversity. Antony explained lifetime does not compare to eternity. Antony became the elder who teaches, just like the elders he learned from. The student became the teacher. Antony encouraged his followers to not surrender to the devil and his evil ways and to increase dedication. He explained a person's lifetime is brief in comparison to eternity, so we should all persevere to enter eternal life. This is about "time" (16).

Then, Antony taught that earth does not compare to Heaven and that we take virtue with us. He told his followers to not lose heart because the earth is small compared to God's Kingdom of Heaven. This is about "space." Antony explained we should surrender earthly treasures through virtue, so we can gain the Kingdom of Heaven. He explained we are going to lose those treasures anyway at death. When we die, we cannot take our possessions with us, but the virtues we develop remain and prepare our way to Heaven (17).

Antony taught that we should master our wills and persist in asceticism. Some may ask if the struggle of the disciplined ascetic life is worth the reward? As the author of this exposition, I hope, at the end, you will agree with me and say "yes" when you learn more about theosis as a sign of Salvation. Antony explained God is Master and we are His servants and if we neglect working for Him, there are negative consequences (18). Antony explained that the Lord is on our side and that we should live as if we are dying. God works for the good of all who choose the good. This should comfort us and give us hope. If we live as people dying daily, we will not commit sin because of the consequences. This is a helpful way to look at life. It is a wise way to look at life that speaks truth because any of us could be dead tomorrow and our eternal fates will be finalized (19).

Antony explained that the task is not external – it is internal. He encouraged his followers to not look back and to continue on the path of virtue. Do we have to travel the world or gain an education to enter God's Kingdom of Heaven? No, because, as Jesus said, "the kingdom of God is in the midst of [or within] you" (Luke 17:21, RSV). The nature of the soul is to keep the soul's path straight intellectually according to its created nature (20).

Adversity

I have chosen to use the word "adversity" to identify the second theme in the masterpiece because it is the best single word to describe Antony's struggles with Satan – the Adversary – and his demons.

At first, the devil tried to stop Antony with worries. He tried to fill Antony's mind with clouds of considerations and ways to lead him away from the discipline (asceticism). However, this did not work, and Antony conquered the devil. The enemy was weak to Antony's resolve, sturdiness, faith and prayers. Then, the devil assumed the form of a woman. The text explains that this is a tactic the devil uses to ambush the young. He attacks the navel of the belly and assumes the form of a woman. Antony conquered these temptations by thinking about Christ and the fire of judgement as well as with God's grace (5). Even so, the devil continued. He revealed himself as the friend of fornication. He did not give up. He pressed harder (6).

It would be foolish to deny the existence of the devil or to consider him a character of fiction. If God exists, so does the adversary, the enemy. Old Testament Scripture refers to the devil and so does Jesus. As 1800s French poet Charles Baudelaire wrote, "The devil's finest trick is to persuade you that he does not exist."

Adversity Continued

When Antony found shelter in the tombs, the devil and his demons beat him up, but then Antony's friend visited him and brought him to the village (8). The author Athanasius explains that Antony's friend visited him by virtue of God's Providence – "for the Lord never overlooks them that hope in Him" (8, Schaff, ccel.org). What is Providence? It is God's protective care or intervention in the universe. What is the devil's role in God's universe? The devil is tempter and deceiver, but the trials help us to make our faith stronger. For those on the right path, the devil's trials bring us closer to God. We realize how much we need God and that God is our only refuge when hit by the devil's storms. The devil is evil, but God uses him to test us and make us better. This can be seen in the story of God, the devil and Job. The devil has influence, but, as we are seeing with Antony, it is weak when compared to the strength that Jesus can empower us with.

Back at the tombs, Antony was attacked, again, by demons who took on the forms of beasts and reptiles (9). However, Antony confronted them with a reasoned response to their attack:

> he said, 'If there had been any power in you, it would have sufficed had one of you come, but since the Lord hath made you weak, you attempt to terrify me by numbers: and a proof of your weakness is that you take the shapes of brute beasts.' And again with boldness he said, 'If you are able, and have received power against me, delay not to attack; but if you are unable, why trouble me in vain? For faith in our Lord is a seal and a wall of safety to us.' So after many attempts they gnashed their teeth upon him, because they were mocking themselves rather than him (9, Schaff, ccel.org).

Then, the Lord gave Antony a sign of reassurance (10):

> Nor was the Lord then forgetful of Antony's wrestling, but was at hand to help him. So looking up he saw the roof as it were opened, and a ray of light descending to him. The

demons suddenly vanished, the pain of his body straightway ceased, and the building was again whole. But Antony feeling the help, and getting his breath again, and being freed from pain, besought the vision which had appeared to him, saying, 'Where wert thou? Why didst thou not appear at the beginning to make my pains to cease?' And a voice came to him, 'Antony, I was here, but I waited to see thy fight; wherefore since thou hast endured, and hast not been worsted, I will ever be a succour to thee, and will make thy name known everywhere.' Having heard this, Antony arose and prayed, and received such strength that he perceived that he had more power in his body than formerly. And he was then about thirty-five years old (10, Schaff, ccel.org).

Some people may question if God truly speaks to us. Surely, sometimes, He does directly. He may speak to us through a voice or through a sign. However, most times, God speaks to us indirectly by others or when we read the Bible.

After God spoke to Antony, the devil tried to tempt Antony with an apparition of a silver dish. However, Antony boldly confronted the devil and dismissed the illusion (11). Then, as he continued to travel to the mountain, Antony was tempted by actual gold, but he ignored the temptation (12). What is money's worth when one is rich with God? Antony had no possessions, and he was battling demons, but he was being blessed by God. With God's favor, this desert man became the father of a new movement bringing countless closer to the Lord.

The author Athanasius referred to Antony as an athlete in training. Antony was a spiritual athlete and a spiritual warrior. At this point, Antony had enough bread for six months, and once he found an abandoned fortress, he received more loaves twice a year. This way of living lasted many years (12). The demons even manifested themselves as an apparition of a mob. This frightened visiting acquaintances, but Antony remained steadfast, and the demons could not harm him (13).

Adversity Continued Further

As I mentioned, in sections 16-43, Athanasius wrote about Antony's discourse around the themes of asceticism and adversity. The source of adversity is Satan – the Adversary – and his demons. Evil spirits are the enemy, but the qualities or powers that lead to death are anger, desire and the other sins. When a Christian uses the phrase "keep watch," he is referring to being alert to when sin and evil attack one's soul (21). We must keep watch of demons' attacks. They are the spirits that fell into darkness. God created everything, and He is the Greatest Good, but some may ask – did God also create demons who are evil? God made them good as angels, but they fell away from heavenly wisdom. We can discriminate the demons' influences on us through the Holy Spirit who we get to know through prayer and asceticism. We can also distinguish between different demons and recognize their traits. Antony attested to this, and we can believe him because he had personally experienced and overcame them (22).

We learn more about the attack of demons and their nature. Antony taught his audience to not fear them because we can defeat them through prayer, fasting, faith in the Lord as well as the sign of the Cross. However, once defeated, demons do not retreat or give up. They attack, again, in another way (23).

Antony continued by describing the devil – his appearance, the environment that he works in and his intentions. The devil is menacing and appears larger than life; he lies and speaks no truth, but Christians have the power to trample him underfoot, and he cannot hinder their asceticism (24).

Demons are treacherous and deceive and even intervene with holy masks, but it is unnecessary to heed them. Their intention is to bring people to despair and to have people believe that the discipline is useless, and they try to make people sick of solitary life (25). Antony explained the demons' ways. Demons intend to confuse, disturb and deceive. They can make crashing and laughing noises and make pretend (26).

Antony taught his audience to emulate holy ones and ignore demons. We counteract the demons and their intentions by emulating holy ones with their courage, by not paying attention to demons as if they are strangers, by not obeying demons, and by being devoted to the discipline. The author Athanasius and the monk Antony were like doctors prescribing ways to remedy ills. They were preparing those who follow them with what to expect and to not fear (27).

The devil and demons have no real power. They are truly weak and are powerless against those who adhere to Christ. Demons only deliver threats. Antony explained the power of a true angel of the Lord compared to the demons. For example, he pointed out 2 Kings 19:35, where it says one true angel had the power to quietly destroy 185,000 foes (28). Antony also pointed out that the devil could not stop Job. In the story of Job, the devil did not possess any real power. This is true because God permitted the devil to test Job, and then God blessed Job with greater abundance. God is the one with the Power, not the devil. So, we, too, should trust God, like Job, even when we suffer from the devil's ways because if we trust God, in the end, we, too, will be blessed with greater abundance (29).

Demons fear ascetics who have Christ on their side. We should not fear the devil and his demons. We should fear God alone. We should hold demons in contempt. Demons fear ascetics because of their virtue and devotion to Christ. We have authority over the enemy because of Jesus, the Savior (30).

Antony explained demons pretend to prophesy but do not know the future. They have no foreknowledge and are rather like thieves who run ahead (31). Demons claim to predict the future but can foretell no more than human beings. Demons run ahead and see things already happening, but if Providence plans differently, demons speak falsely (32). The Lord is more powerful than demons. Even if demons seem to speak the truth, we should not listen since they cannot prophesy. Furthermore, knowing the future is not a blessing and does not save. Faith saves. Knowing the future does not produce virtue or represent a good character. Rather than foretelling the future, we should be concerned with faith and observing the commandments (33). We should live holy lives, and if we are given foresight, we will see clearly. A person with a pure soul can see more clearly than demons. This is possible through the Lord (34).

Antony taught his audience to ignore evil spirits and embrace holy spirits and that God will guide them to discriminate. He said that holy spirits bring peace, tranquility and delight to the soul without necessarily bringing disturbance. With the power of God the Father, courage enters the soul, which looks forward to future divine realities. A vision of a holy spirit can sometimes bring fear upon a person because the soul is in the presence of a superior holy being, but holy spirits remove fear through love (35). Antony explained how to discern evil spirits from holy spirits: evil trouble and terrorize the soul, but you know you are in the presence of holiness if fear is instantly removed and replaced with joy, strength, calmness and the love of God (36). When in the presence of superior beings – holy angels remove fear, but wicked demons terrify further. A couple of examples of holy angels removing fear include Archangel Gabriel for the Virgin Mother Mary and the angel for the women at Jesus's tomb. On the contrary, wicked demons say, "fall down and worship me" (Matthew 4:9, RSV) (37).

    Antony taught his audience to not be proud of their ability to overcome demons because it is not them, it is the Lord's power. We should not boast about expelling demons because the performance is the Savior's work. Rather than wanting to expel demons, we should be concerned with our virtue (38).

    Antony explained his teachings were from personal experience and his own battles with demons (39). He provided examples of his battles with demons. He defeated a very tall demon claiming to be the power of God by mentioning the name of Christ. Demons have even taken on the appearances of monks. Antony resisted the demonic illusion of gold by singing the Psalms. Demonic whippings never separated Antony from the love of Christ (40). Exasperated, Satan himself confronted Antony. Satan asked why Christians censure and curse him, and then he confessed his own weakness. Christians with Christ are stronger than Satan himself because of the Savior (41). The devil himself is weak against those who walk with Christ. We should not fear and rather rejoice. If the evil one confessed to Antony his weakness, we should treat the evil one with utter contempt for his unrelenting wickedness. We should not despair when demons attack. We should react, instead, with courage and always rejoice because the Lord is with us. Demons battle us by corresponding to our condition, and they pattern their phantasms after our thoughts. However, if our minds are filled with thoughts of Christ, demons can do nothing. A healthy state of mind despises the enemy, and with the Lord, it rejoices in hope (42).

Antony advised his audience to put spirits to the test by asking them who they are. The holy ones will bring joy, and your fear will turn to joy. The evil ones will be weakened by your bravery and calmness. Remember, Athanasius put on paper this advice from Antony as an instruction manual for spiritual warriors (43).

Chrysostom on Adversity

You should know that adversity and suffering are unavoidable. Orthodox Holy Hierarch and Catholic Doctor of the Church Saint John Chrysostom (the Golden Mouth) – in Discourse III, chiefly on the parable of the rich man and Lazarus – teaches at length that suffering is inescapable. I will cite a brief excerpt from section 6:

> As therefore, of those who commit sin, they who suffer no ill here, undergo greater punishment hereafter; thus also, of those who live righteously, they who suffer many ills here, enjoy greater honour there. And if there be two sinners, the one punished here, the other not punished; the one who is punished is more fortunate than the one unpunished. Again, if there be two righteous men, of whom one endures more, and the other fewer trials; he that endures the most is the most fortunate, since to each will be rendered according to his work.
>
> What then? Is it not possible, they say, to enjoy ease both here and hereafter? This, O man, is unattainable; it is one of the things impossible. It cannot, it cannot be, that he who here enjoys ease and plenty, and continually indulges in every luxury----who lives a vain and aimless life----can also enjoy honour hereafter. At the same time, if he be not troubled by poverty, he still is troubled by desire, and from this cause suffers restraint---- a cause which gives rise to no small amount of trouble, Again, if disease do not afflict him, yet evil passion burns within, and it is no

slight pain that springs from wrath; also, if trials be not laid upon him, yet wicked thoughts |76 constantly arise to vex him. It is by no means a trivial matter to restrain lawless desire, to put a stop to vainglorious thoughts, to check insensate pride, to refrain from excess, to live in self-denial. And he who does not accomplish these things, and such as these, can never attain salvation (ccel.org).

So, some people might ask if it is possible to not suffer at all. And, Saint John Chrysostom makes it very clear that this is not possible. At some point, we all shall suffer. Furthermore, in the Lord's Prayer, Jesus taught us to ask God the Father to "lead us not into temptation, / But deliver us from evil [or the evil one]" (Matthew 6:13). As we should pray the Lord's Prayer often, this shows us our constant battle with temptation and evil. In the evening prayers prescribed by the Orthodox Christian Church, the Christian is advised to ask the Lord our God to "deliver me from all influence and temptation of the evil one" and to "deliver us from all tribulation, evil and distress." These prayers are to be used every night. We must combat evil every day. And, we can overcome the devil and his influence – which leads to suffering – if we walk with Jesus Christ. Those that defeat the devil attain theosis and enter a divine state through Jesus Christ. This is victory. This is

Salvation. And, this will be reviewed in the following sections.

More on Asceticism Against the Devil

Some may ask, "Why practice asceticism, if the devil is going to attack?" In short, the devil will attack regardless, but asceticism is the only method to conquering the devil. We learn from Gospels Matthew (chapter 17), Mark (chapter 9) and Luke (chapter 9) that Jesus cured a boy with a demon. No one else – including the disciples – could cure the boy. Depending on which Gospel's perspective and which translation is read, Jesus explained that a demon like this never comes out except by faith, prayer and fasting – in one word, asceticism. We will see this clearly through our Antony who cast out demons with his theosis through Jesus Christ.

Some may say asceticism leads to madness and visions of the devil. In fact, the opposite is true. It leads to clarity of mind and simplicity of lifestyle. It strengthens people as they travel to God. The Bible and the Church Fathers often use an analogy to describe the soul's purification. They say it is like gold refined in a furnace fire. This is very true for Antony, monastics and all Christians through the process of asceticism and the trials from adversity. The soul is valuable – like gold – and when put through the furnace fires of asceticism and adversity, the soul is purified as undesirable qualities are purged.

Asceticism is detachment from worldly ways. The devil's schemes are most obvious when we are not entangled in worldly ways. If we remove worldly distraction and clear the fog in our minds, then the devil's wickedness is more obvious. The devil's influence and temptations are constantly present. Whether we are distracted or not, as long as we are alive, the devil will continue to agitate and trouble us. However, we are more aware of the devil and his ways when we are purifying ourselves as we do through asceticism. The advantage for us in this is that we are not as easily fooled when we are in a state of purification and so can combat his wily ways more successfully. So, with asceticism, the ruses of the devil seem more numerous but that is only because the ascetic is more aware and this, in fact, is the first true step in defeating the devil. Knowing is half the battle and is the only path that leads to victory, so do not be fooled or weakened by laziness or reluctancy – that is what the devil wants, and he does not want what is best for you. God wants what is best for you, so follow Him and the saints – like Antony – who have reached Him.

The devil attacks most directly at those who are closest to the Lord. He wants to weaken the relationship between God and His elect. The devil envies the relationship and is jealous of the love shared. He wants the same loyalty, but his ego, pride and self-centeredness spoil any type of meaningful relationship because he does not care about anyone – he cares only for himself. God loves you, so develop a relationship with God. Follow the lead of His saints who have testified about His Love.

Second Half

Theosis

This section on theosis only makes sense and has relevance when considering the sections on asceticism and adversity. The previous sections show how Antony was able to get to the divine state of theosis. At the conclusion of Antony's discourse about asceticism and adversity, the themes of Athanasius's masterpiece shift. By the time we reach the end of the discourse at section 43, the topics of asceticism and adversity have been well treated and the second half of the masterpiece begins. In the text, there continues to be mention of asceticism but not as much. Antony continues his ascetic lifestyle and he continues to battle adversity from demons, but now the theme of theosis emerges. Antony conquered the devil with Christ which led to theosis – the Greek term for deification and divinization (being made divine). We learn what is theosis and what is theosis's power. The following part of the second half of the masterpiece is apologetic writings in defense of Christianity which is an aspect of theosis.

After Antony's discourse, his audience rejoiced, virtue increased, carelessness was discarded, conceit ended, demons were hated, and the Lord was marveled. The desert – which was first inhabited by Antony – became a city of monks. All are instances of the beginnings of theosis (44). For Antony, the soul had higher priority than the body. Antony was ashamed by the body's necessities and thought we should devote all our time to the soul instead of the body (45).

We learn that Antony was provoked to leave his cell in the desert because Christians were being martyred. He desired martyrdom for himself, and during this outing, he remained with the martyrs until they were perfected. However, it appears the Lord protected Antony, so he could teach the discipline and be an example for others (46). When the persecution ended, Antony withdrew again to his cell to practice more strenuous asceticism – always fasting, living in meager clothing and no bathing (47).

Antony directed visitors to faith in Christ. He helped many; although, some were a nuisance to him, such as with a certain military officer who sought out Antony on behalf of his daughter who was possessed by a demon. Nonetheless, great numbers received great benefit from Antony, and he helped them through his living example. Many were cleansed when they believed and prayed with sincerity (48).

For quiet and out of humility, Antony departed from his cell away from the multitude who were visiting him. His personal reasons for leaving were that he thought he might become prideful or others might think more of him because of the Lord's works through him. He was guided during his departure by a heavenly voice from above. He traveled to a new land and ended up on a high hill with water below and date palms that were a bit further away (49). At his new home, Antony got to work planting crops with tools brought by monks. He plowed the land and planted vegetables. However, after this work, he faced a problem. Beasts damaged the crops. Antony – now in the state of theosis – told the beasts to leave in the name of the Lord and this resolved the problem (50).

As Antony grew old, the demons did not give up and they did not stop attacking him. He overcame the demons by kneeling before, praying to and trusting in the Lord. He also made peace with the wild beasts (51). Then the devil sent wild hyenas emerging from their dens to confront Antony, but Antony – in theosis – conquered them by announcing his devotion to Christ (52). Even though Antony was alone and old in the desert, the demons did not have any power over him. A demonic beast appeared but fled, fell and died when Antony announced his allegiance to Christ. The beast's demons also were left powerless by Antony's devotion to Christ (53).

One time, the monks convinced Antony to return with them to oversee them for a bit. As they were traveling, they ran out of water. Antony prayed, and the Lord miraculously made water gush forth. When they completed the trip, everyone embraced Antony as a father and joy returned to the mountains. Antony also reunited with his sister who was now old, as well (54).

After a few days with people, Antony returned to the mountain. The people followed him, and he delivered a message just like those he delivered in the past. He told them to have faith, not sin, recount their actions, do good, have compassion, have no impure thoughts, please the Lord and trample the enemy (55). Antony prayed to God for all who were suffering and for all who approached him. Did God answer every prayer for every person? God acts as He wishes. Even so, all who visited and received Antony's prayers learned to be patient and give thanks to God alone (56).

Sections 57-64 are mostly about the Lord healing people through Antony's theosis. For example, a man suffering was healed as Antony proclaimed. The suffering man bit his own tongue and was about to lose his eyes but was healed when he visited Antony. Why was he healed? The man was healed because of his faith (57). Then, a girl with a hideous ailment was healed. The young woman – who was filled with mucus that turned to worms, whose body was paralyzed and whose eyes were defective – asked Antony to pray for her to be healed, and she was then healed. Why was she healed? She was healed because of her faith in the Lord (58).

There were times when Antony had visions of distant happenings, such as with two brothers who ran out of water where one died and the other was waiting to die. Antony was able to help save people without seeing them physically as when the one brother was revived with water, while the other brother died as according to God's judgement. This was possible because the Lord showed Antony distant happenings (59).

Then, we learn about a monk's death, and a story of a miracle from the past resurfaced. God worked wonders through other monks – not only through Antony – like when the monk Amun was transported across a flooded river. This was made possible by the Lord. We discover Antony saw a vision from a great distance of monk Amun's death – when his soul was led up into the air. Antony's vision was possible because of the purity of his soul. The accuracy of his vision was confirmed by his fellow monks who visited him (60).

Some may question if these types of events are possible, and I tell you anything is possible with God. This is clear with the miracle of Jesus's Resurrection, which was confirmed by his disciples who saw him in flesh and bones after his death. These disciples were tortured and killed and never let go of their witnesses and testimonies. They are the basis for the authenticity of Jesus's miraculous Resurrection, and if Jesus can Rise from the dead, then we should be open to the possibility that anything is possible with the Lord.

Through holy men like Antony, God can work miracles immediately, as He did with the Christ-inspired maiden Polycratia who was freed from ascetic pains at the moment of Antony's prayer for her (61). Antony helped many and always asked to not marvel at him but the Lord – since the Lord was the source of his theosis. Antony could predict things in advance, as he often predicted those who would visit him and their reasons for visiting. By what measure – to what extent – are people shown favor by the Lord? In the measure of their capacity for knowing him; namely, by the level of their faith (62).

Antony even sensed the stench of a demon's odor (63). We also learn that a man possessed by a demon was made well by the Lord through Antony's word. Demons can be truly hideous and disgusting on those they possess, as was the case with a possessed nobleman who devoured his bodily excrement. However, we learn that when people are battling their demons, the people are not at fault; rather, it is the demons who are at fault (64).

Antony was accused about his life from demons, but from the time he became a monk, the demons could only create lies. Antony had a wonderful out of body vision of celestial beings defending his life from foul beings. When a person becomes a monk, God wipes clean his life from birth, and he begins a new life. The demons were not able to accuse Antony of any evil since he became a monk (65). Even though Antony was old and experienced in spiritual warfare and successful as a virtuous monk, the evil spirits did not stop. Life until death is a struggle even for the best of us. And, the only means of true relief is Jesus Christ.

Antony also received spiritual favor and visions, which encouraged him to strive for what lies ahead. Antony had a providential vision about the soul's passage after this life. He saw the enemy – who was huge and reaching to the clouds – prevent the passage of souls and rejoice, but the enemy gnashed his teeth at the souls who ascended and passed him. This vision caused Antony to strive to what lies ahead. Visions can frequently take the place as an assuagement – a making less severe – of the trials we face (66).

Antony was blessed with a stable character and a pure soul. Antony never became arrogant because of his divine strength and the attention of the people. Rather, he was tolerant, humble and honored the Church. Antony stood out in a crowd. His face expressed grace from the Savior. He was cheerful, calm, never gloomy, joyous (67).

Theosis Continued

Powerful rulers wrote to Antony, but he was unimpressed. Nonetheless, he counselled them, and they rejoiced. Antony attracted and was influential with all kinds of people when he was alive – including rulers. However, he did not make a great deal of the rulers' letters. Antony told the rulers to not count present realities as great and that Christ alone is true and eternal ruler. They reacted favorably to Antony, and he was held in affection by everyone as a father (81).

Antony had a vision of mules – representing the Arian heretics – attacking the Church's altar. Antony went into ecstasy from the terrible vision. In it, mules were kicking rebelliously in the Church's altar which was a prophecy fulfilled two years later of the Arian assault and their senseless teachings (82).

Antony was one example of a true miraculous life in Christ the Savior (83). Antony cured by the power of Christ. When Antony healed, the power came from Christ. His part in bringing about the miracles was his prayers and the discipline – which are key elements in attaining theosis. Even the judges requested his help. The judges learned from Antony to value justice and fear God. The people sought out Antony, but rather than a life among the people, he preferred the discipline in the mountain. Antony loved his way of life in the mountain (84). Antony needed the mountain, silence and the discipline – like a fish needs water. Antony explained that a monk away from the mountain and his discipline is like a fish out of water, so the monk must return. Because of Antony's analogy, the people marveled at his intellect and called him a servant of God who is loved by God (85).

Antony foretold the wrath against Balacius, a wicked military commander. Balacius beat virgins and monks, and Antony wrote him a letter foreseeing wrath upon him. Later, Balacius was bitten and attacked by his horse then died (86).

Antony did so much good and helped so many people in Egypt that the author Athanasius likened him to a physician given to Egypt by God. He was like God's physician who healed all kinds of people in Egypt (87). All who came to Antony benefited from him – demons' plots were overturned, women remained virgins, foreigners saw him as a father (88).

Christian Apologetics

One significant aspect of theosis is the divine wisdom and holy ability to defend the Christian Faith. This method of thought and the literature that grew from it is known as apologetics. The term apologetics does not mean to apologize, as if to say, "I'm sorry." Apologetics writing is a defense:

Typically, these consisted of what are called negative apologetics, wherein a writer takes up a series of challenges to Christian belief and shows them to lack the power that their proponents think they have.

We also sometimes see positive apologetics, an argument that attempts to provide its audience with some fresh positive reasons for belief, intended to convince others who are not yet convinced of the truth of the Christian faith (Mathewes, "Books That Matter: The City of God," *The Great Courses* Guidebook: 87).

Sections 68-80 is primarily Christian apologetics. Antony embraced Orthodoxy and rejected heresy. The word orthodox comes from the Greek and means correct belief. Antony never held communion with heretics and abhorred heresy (68). He condemned the Arian heretics and proclaimed truth about the Son of God. Arians said the Son was a creature from nonbeing; when according to Orthodoxy, the Son is the Eternal Word coexistent with the Father (69). People rejoiced at Antony's proclamations and his condemnation of heretics. The people called him "the man of God" (70, Schaff, ccel.org) (70).

We learn that a mother's child was delivered from a demon through Antony by the power of Christ (71).

Next, two philosophers visited Antony. As we have seen, Antony was a holy man who conquered demons and a righteous man who was a servant of God. Even though he was not formally educated, he was wise. He proved he was wiser than the two Greek philosophers who visited him. Antony asked them why they were visiting him if they believed he was a foolish man, and he told them that if he was wise, they should become as he was and become Christians (72).

Antony was not educated, but his mind was sound, and his demeanor was civil. He was praised. To defend himself from others who ridiculed his lack of education, Antony explained and showed that the mind is the inventor of letters and that a man whose mind is sound does not need letters. They marveled at his untrained understanding. Because of his speech, people saw him as gracious and civil. No one resented him, and all who came to him rejoiced over him (73).

Antony defended the Christian Faith to the Greeks who were considered wise. He compared the Christian courage of the Cross and disdain for death against pagan lewdness and the debauchery of their gods. He also compared Christians believing Christ making them divine against pagans worshipping creatures (74). Antony continued his defense of

Christianity. He compared the bravery of the Cross and confronting death against the mad myths of the Greek gods. Antony asked why pagans mock the Cross but are silent about miracles and signs which reveal that Christ is God (75). Antony condemned the foolishness of the Greek gods and the Greeks who worshipped the created order instead of God who did the Creating (76).

Antony stumped the so-called wise men. He showed them faith in God from within the soul is more secure than their dialectic and demonstrated arguments (77). Power of one's faith in Christ is more secure than Greek word battles (78). The power of Christ's Cross puts the spells of other beliefs to shame (79). Faith in Christ is the true Faith. It heals and banishes demons which Greek word play and magic cannot. The philosophers who visited Antony were persuaded by him (80).

I believe Antony's Christian apologetics – his defense – continues to be as persuasive today as it was when he spoke it over 1500 years ago. The final theme illustrated in the masterpiece is not apologetics. Athanasius crafted a wonderful biography of Antony that returns to the theme of Antony's theosis. After we discover more examples of Antony's theosis, we learn about the end of his earthly life.

Antony's Death

Antony sensed his own death and counselled his brother monks. Antony was 105 years old when he sensed his own death, and the monks wept when Antony told them that it was approaching. However, Antony was cheerful (89). Antony explained to his brother monks the importance of burying the body. The Egyptians took care of the bodies of their worthy dead. They wrapped them and kept them inside but did not bury them. Christians should bury the bodies of their departed as was done to the Lord's body when it was laid in the tomb (90).

Antony became ill and gave the two men with him his final instructions about life as a Christian monk and his own burial. Antony got ill a few months after his foresight to death. Antony encouraged the two monks to stay enthusiastic in the discipline and find inspiration in Christ. He told them again (sections 89 & 91) to "live as though dying daily" (91, Schaff, ccel.org). He told them to stay away from the schismatics and Arians and find allies among themselves, the Lord and the saints. Then, he told them to bury his body in the earth where no one else would know where. Antony gave to Bishop Athanasius – who is the author of the masterpiece – the sheepskin and the cloak that he lay on – which were first gifted new to him by Athanasius (91). Antony's face, as he died, seemed bright. After death, his body was buried. His only possessions, which he gave away as gifts, were cared for like great treasures (92).

Antony is remembered as a great holy man of God. Antony never succumbed to extravagances, even in old age. Antony's health until the time of death was injury free – he saw clearly, kept teeth, had healthy feet and hands. After death, the one thing Antony was acclaimed for was religion. Even though he lived a solitary life in the Egyptian desert, Antony's fame reached far to Spain, Gaul, Rome, Africa. The author Athanasius said this was possible because God makes his people known and shows them like lamps to everyone (93). The author Athanasius believed his work about Antony's life should be read to learn true monasticism and the glory given to those who glorify Christ and that with Christ, the demons have no power (94).

More Theology on Theosis

Irenaeus on Theosis

Theosis has been lived out by the Church's great mystics and has been investigated by the Church's greatest theologians. Church Father Saint Irenaeus contributed to Christian theology and identified how theosis is a result of redemption.

What is redemption? The word redeem means to compensate for defects or wrongs as well as to save. It means to be put right with or even to recover, regain or get back. So, what is Christian Redemption? It means to be redeemed by God through Jesus Christ. Christian Redemption means to be saved through Jesus Christ from sin, death and hell. Redemption through Jesus Christ is Salvation.

Saint Irenaeus talks about Recapitulation Theology, which is one form of Redemption Theology. It illustrates how we are put in good standing with God. It is based on Scripture. What does recapitulate mean? Recapitulate means to sum up or repeat. The word recap has the same definition. Recapitulation Redemption Theology teaches that Jesus renews us and reverses Adam's error. The Most Holy Virgin Mother Mary has an important role in this theology.

Irenaeus explains how "The New Creation in Christ 'Recapitulates' the Old" (Richardson, *Early Christian Fathers*, "Irenaeus," ccel.org. 333). In his theology, he illustrates the recapitulation of Adam by Jesus:

- Adam is disobedient to God by a tree (the tree of the knowledge of good and evil). Jesus is obedient to God by a tree (the wood Cross).
- Virgin Eve, betrothed to a man (Adam), is seduced. Virgin Mary, betrothed to a man (Joseph), is blessed.

- Through an evil angel (Satan), Eve flees from and rebels against God. Through a holy angel (Gabriel), Mary obeys God.
- Eve disobeys God and falls. Mary obeys God to become the advocate of Eve.
- Human race is subjected to death by a virgin. Human race is saved by a virgin.
- Sin of Adam (the first-formed) is amended by the chastisement of Jesus (the First-begotten).
- Wisdom of a serpent (evil, sin) is conquered by simplicity of the dove (peace, holiness, Holy Spirit).
- Through this recapitulation, the chains were broken by which we were in bondage to death.

Redemption through recapitulation by Jesus leads to theosis – also known as deification and divinization (being made divine). Jesus makes us divine as we were meant to be before Adam and Eve's Fall. With Jesus, humankind can return to Paradise.

Further Theology on Theosis

As I mentioned in the introduction, Saint Irenaeus said, God had "become what we are, that He might bring us to be even what He is Himself" (*Against Heresies: Book V*, "Preface," ccel.org). This event occurred in the Incarnation where God and humankind united in the person of Jesus Christ who was born of the Holy Spirit and the Virgin Mary. Jesus was fully God and fully human and formed a bridge, so humankind can reach God Almighty. Many theologians have said that the union of God and man in the person of Jesus Christ allows humankind to enjoy a closer union with God and be more like God than Adam and Eve were in the Garden of Eden. Through Jesus Christ, humankind is not only able to be restored to its divine state, but it also reaches its fullest divine potential. Theosis is meant to be the goal of every human life. Through sinless Jesus Christ, a sinner is able to be reconciled with Holy God. If we want theosis, we must follow Jesus Christ and do what he taught us to do. We must repent for our sins and pray to our Gracious God for mercy. Theosis arises from an internal transformation of mind, heart and soul; and only from an internal transformation can the external be transformed, as we see with our Antony and the miraculous wonders worked through his theosis.

    To be clear – God Almighty is Uncreated, Timeless, Limitless, Infinite, Incomprehensible. Eastern Orthodox Christian theology teaches that humankind cannot share God's unapproachable essence; however, humankind can have communion and union with God through a synergy (cooperation) with His divine energies. We can partake in the Father's divine energies through following the example of the Son and by being a living temple for the Holy Spirit. Orthodoxy teaches that while in the state of theosis, the mystic – like our Antony – takes on God-like divine qualities yet retains his personal characteristics. The human being who is blessed with theosis is a god by grace but remains an individual person. Theosis can occur in this life, but it will only be fully and eternally realized in the Resurrection with "a new heaven and a new earth" (Revelation 21:1). Theologians can investigate the process of theosis; however, as we see with our Antony, theosis is not an academic pursuit but a transformative result made possible through asceticism and a holy Christian life. Christian theology is rich, dense and deep. It can be as basic as "love your neighbor as yourself" (Matthew 22:39, RSV) and as intense as theosis.

Even so, the mysteries of the Almighty are revealed to those who search. Jesus teaches us, "seek, and you will find" (Matthew 7:7, RSV), and we should follow his teachings because he is "the way, and the truth, and the life" and "no one comes to the Father, but by [him]" (Matthew John 14:6, RSV). In this present age (and, perhaps, in every age since the fall of humankind), truth is not widely prized. Deception has become the means to worldly power; however, there is an unconquerable power beyond this world with the Almighty. For those who desire this heavenly reward, seek and you will find, and I can attest that you will find truth in Jesus Christ.

At this moment, permit me a paragraph to clarify the theological context of my theological treatise "Agape into Eternity," which is about immortality, union with God and eternal life. I believe this is a fine opportunity to elaborate on the treatise and an elaboration that has value for the student of theology and anyone who is curious about what is after the death of the mortal body. When I wrote my theological treatise "Agape into Eternity," I was primarily thinking about the mysterious time period after death and before the Resurrection. Not the state of theosis taught in the Church of a saint such as our Antony, who attained theosis while alive and then to be fully realized with the Resurrection of the dead at the Final Judgement. I was primarily thinking about the mysterious middle time period when the soul is separated from the body in Paradise – as expressed when our Lord and Savior Jesus Christ is dying on the Cross and tells the repenting thief, "Truly, I say to you, today you will be with me in Paradise" (Luke 23:43, RSV). God is Agape Love, and union with God in this place of Paradise is eternal unmitigated bliss in agape love. It is something we should all hope for and look forward to. This is more thoroughly investigated in my book *In the Name of Salvation* in the treatise "Agape into Eternity." For those interested, please seek out the treatise. To attain theosis as well as eternal life, we need faith, hope and love (agape). And, since the greatest is love (agape), then we must inquire and seek out Jesus Christ because no human being had more love (agape) than Jesus Christ – as exemplified in his life, teachings and death.

Conclusion

Through this exposition, I hope the reader is better able to see, identify and understand the themes in Athanasius's *Life of Antony*. I hope the reader can see how asceticism is used to combat adversity from the evil one and his demons as well as see how victory – through Christian asceticism – leads to theosis, which is the goal of Christian life. Antony was a human being just like us, and if he could do it, we all can. I pray this work leads the reader at least one step closer to Jesus Christ and theosis. Amen.

Bibliography and Works Cited

Introduction:
- Clebsch, William A. "Preface." *Athanasius – The Life of Antony and the Letter to Marcellinus*. Paulist Press: 1980.
- Gregg, Robert C. "Introduction." *Athanasius – The Life of Antony and the Letter to Marcellinus*. Paulist Press: 1980.

Life of Antony Translation:

When summarizing the masterpiece, I paraphrased from…

- Gregg, Robert C. (translator). *Athanasius – The Life of Antony and the Letter to Marcellinus*. Paulist Press: 1980.

When quoting the masterpiece, I cited from…

- Schaff, Philip (editor). *Athanasius: Life of Antony*. Christian Classics Ethereal Library: https://www.ccel.org. Accessed 10-21-2020.

Chrysostom on Adversity:

- John Chrysostom. *Four Discourses, chiefly on the parable of the rich man and Lazarus – Discourse III*. Christian Classics Ethereal Library: https://www.ccel.org. Accessed 10-21-2020.

Christian Apologetics:

- Mathewes, Charles. "Books That Matter: The City of God." *The Great Courses* DVD Course with Guidebook. The Teaching Company: 2016.

More Theology on Theosis:

- Irenaeus. *Against Heresies: Book V*. Christian Classics Ethereal Library: https://www.ccel.org. Accessed 10-21-2020.
- Richardson, Cyril C (editor). *Early Christian Fathers – Selections from the Work Against Heresies by Irenaeus, Bishop of Lyons*. Christian Classics Ethereal Library: https://www.ccel.org. Accessed 10-21-2020.

- Ware, Timothy (Kallistos). *The Orthodox Church: An Introduction to Eastern Christianity*. Penguin Books: 2015.
- Wikipedia.org. *Theosis (Eastern Christian theology)*. Accessed 10-21-2020.

MASTERPIECE: Anonymously authored *The Way of a Pilgrim*

TITLE OF EXPOSITION: Praying Unceasingly as Holy Life

Description

The anonymously authored *The Way of a Pilgrim* is a masterpiece that is part story and part instruction manual on prayer. The pilgrim may be the main character, but the story is nothing without the Jesus Prayer. This exposition is an analysis of unceasing prayer as taught in *The Way of a Pilgrim*. Considered the "art of arts" and "science of sciences," prayer makes it possible for a person to endure and embrace life's struggles – through God's grace – as the only way to happiness in this fallen world on the way to Heaven. Enjoy and may God bless you.

Contents

+ Introduction
+ *The Way of a Pilgrim* Analysis
+ Conclusion
    + The Pilgrim
    + Theosis and Hesychia
    + Psyche
    + Final Thoughts
+ Bibliography and Works Cited

Introduction

The Way of a Pilgrim's origin is mysterious. Scholars are not sure if it is a true story by the narrator, a first-person account of another pilgrim(s)'s journey(s), or a fictional story created to teach the reader about the Eastern Orthodox Christian method of how to pray the Jesus Prayer. The masterpiece was authored anonymously; however, we do know that it is a Russian work written in the 19th century.

The book teaches us that life is communion with God and that unceasing prayer to God leads to life. It teaches us that life is only possible through Jesus and that praying his name makes union with God possible. The pilgrim learned this in the context of the Orthodox Church with his most treasured Bible as he wandered around Russia to learn from others.

He took each adventure one step at a time – moment by moment – and his only constants were the Jesus Prayer and his books. He discovered the writings of Orthodox Christian spiritual masters that are collected in an anthology known as the *Philokalia* – translated in English as "love of the beautiful, the good." The *Philokalia* teaches the reader about unceasing interior prayer, specifically the Jesus Prayer. *The Way of a Pilgrim* can be seen as an introduction to or key highlights of the Jesus Prayer in the *Philokalia*. *The Way of a Pilgrim* is part story and part instruction manual on prayer. The pilgrim may be the main character, but the story is nothing without the Jesus Prayer.

    Through his experiences, the pilgrim taught us that unceasing prayer in the name of Jesus is only possible within the framework of Christian Church and its experienced teachers. Practicing the prayer outside the Church will be fruitless and will only lead to spiritual delusion. The prayer relies on personal responsibility as well as guidance from experienced teachers in the Church, such as a spiritual elder – in Greek, geronda and in Russian, starets.

    In Eastern Orthodox Christian monasticism, the Jesus Prayer is a vital part of life. However, the Jesus Prayer is not only for monks. As illustrated in *The Way of a Pilgrim*, it is also for lay Christians who seek an intimate relationship and union with God. Inner prayer and spiritual life are for all of us. Even so, it is crucial for the lay Christian to be a faithful participant in the Church and seek the guidance of a spiritual father.

Like Orthodox Christian monastics and the pilgrim, I have discovered the value of the Jesus Prayer. I have applied it to my life and have reaped its benefits. I may not live in a monastery with a community of monks and I may not be a wanderer like the pilgrim; however, for most of my adulthood, I have considered myself to be a religious Christian ascetic. I spent the early part of my adulthood in search of wisdom, truth and God; and I found Jesus Christ to be the way, the truth and the life to God the Father. As a baptized Orthodox Christian, I regularly worship in church during the Sunday Liturgy and during the high holy days. I fast from meat and dairy twice a week – every Wednesday and Friday – throughout the year as prescribed by the Orthodox Church. I am attracted to women, but I abstain from sex and guard myself from lust. The first thing I do after I wake up in the morning is pray, and the last thing I do before I sleep at night is pray. Two or three times a year I visit my spiritual father to whom I give confession. I love and look forward to receiving the Eucharist. I read the Bible and the writings of the saints. I study, write about and teach Christian theology. I perform the sign of the Cross on myself throughout the day and pray the Jesus Prayer without ceasing. I am very religious and am far from perfect, and it is because I am not perfect that I am so religious.

I trained myself through books and practice to learn the Jesus Prayer and how to apply it to my life. The Jesus Prayer is the second most powerful prayer and is preceded only by the Lord's Prayer (the Our Father), which was formulated by God the Son. The Jesus Prayer began to take form even during Jesus's ministry on earth. In the Gospel of Luke, a blind beggar near Jericho cried out, "Jesus, Son of David, have mercy on me!" Then, he requested to receive his sight. And, Jesus said to him, "Receive your sight; your faith has made you well." Immediately the man received his sight and followed Jesus, glorifying God. And, all the people, when they saw it, gave praise to God, as well (Luke 18:35-43, RSV). Here, we see, even during Jesus's earthly life, his saving power and the origins of the Jesus Prayer. ("Son of David" identifies Jesus as the Messiah [the Christ] because – as prophesied in the Hebrew Scriptures [the Old Testament] – the Messiah is a descendant of Jewish King David. Jesus fulfills this prophecy). Saint Ignatius Brianchaninov pointed out that the Jesus Prayer "is a divine institution... by the Son of God and God Himself" (*On the Prayer of Jesus*, 3). He cited Jesus who said to the apostles, "Whatever you ask in my name, I will do it, that the Father may be glorified in the Son; if you ask anything in my name, I will do it" (John 14:13, RSV). And, when Jesus said, "Truly, truly, I say to you, if you ask anything of the Father, he will give it to you in my name. Hitherto you have asked nothing in my name; ask, and you will receive, that your joy may be full" (John 16:23, RSV). Saint Ignatius also cited (*On the Prayer of Jesus*, 8-9) Apostle Paul who explained that Christ Jesus "humbled himself and became obedient unto death, even death on a cross. Therefore God has highly exalted him and bestowed on him the name which is above every name, that at the name of Jesus every knee should bow, in heaven and on earth and under the earth" (Philippians 2:8, RSV).

The standard version of the Jesus Prayer is – "Lord Jesus Christ, Son of God, have mercy on me, a sinner."

- "Lord" identifies Divinity.
- "Jesus" is derived from the Hebrew Yeshua, which means Savior.
- "Christ" is the Greek term for the Hebrew term Messiah, which means Anointed One – as in God's Anointed Priest-King.
- "Son" identifies the Second Person of the Holy Trinity.
- "of God" identifies the Son's Father.
- "have mercy" identifies dependent humankind's relationship with our Gracious God.
- "on me" makes the prayer personal – I who am praying.

- "a sinner" identifies who I am – it is confession and repentance from a created and fallen human being.

The single short Jesus Prayer is profoundly deep because it defines who is Lord, who we are and our relationship with Him. The Lord is our Master who is above us, and we are created to serve Him here below. With a few words, the prayer shows our reliance upon Him. He is All-Powerful, and only through Him can we be saved from ourselves and the devil in this fallen world. With the prayer, one seeks to repair the breach between God and humankind that began with Eve and Adam's self-centered disobedience. With the prayer, one seeks to reconcile oneself with God. Bishop Kallistos (Timothy) Ware pointed out (*The Orthodox Way*, 38) that the prayer is Trinitarian and that the Holy Spirit also is active when we say this prayer because, as Apostle Paul explained, "no one can say 'Jesus is Lord' except by the Holy Spirit" (1 Corinthians 12:3b, RSV). Each member of the Holy Trinity – God as Father, Son and Holy Spirit – is present in the Jesus Prayer.

Throughout the day as I repeat the Jesus Prayer, I may emphasize and adjust different words, so the prayer takes on varied forms. Oftentimes, in heavenly joy, I sing and repeat, "Lord have mercy" (also, in Greek, "Kyrie eleison") over and over because I cannot adequately handle God's grace. Other times, when I fall into error, I may say, "Oh,

Jesus Christ, I'm so sorry, my Lord. Have mercy." And, for much time, I pray for us all collectively with, "Have mercy on all of us who love you, Jesus Christ." In short, the prayer is flexible; however, the standard version is the perfect expression. It has been used for centuries by great holy men and women. I always return – like a boomerang and magnetic attraction – to the standard version: "Lord Jesus Christ, Son of God, have mercy on me, a sinner." Because I repeat the Jesus Prayer throughout the day, I find myself in constant dialogue with God. And that is the point – prayer is dialogue with God. This is the key to unlocking the mystery of prayer. Unceasing prayer means constant dialogue with God, so you can always be connected to God, so you can become one with God and attain theosis (divinization – being made divine). This process is made possible with the Jesus Prayer – which is why learning the methods of how to use the Jesus Prayer are so important.

   The Jesus Prayer is not merely a meditative mantra that soothes, but more so, it is a petition to a personal God. Repetition of the Jesus Prayer is not a magical means to spiritual peace. It is not an incantation or a spell. It is not a hypnotic chant that will sedate the practitioner. As Bishop Ware explained, "Its object is not relaxation but alertness, not waking slumber but living prayer" (*The Orthodox Way*, 122). It is life in communion with the Holy Spirit that presupposes a pure, attentive, faithful and loving life. It is a private call to God. It is an invocation addressed to our personal God and petition for His help to bring us to spiritual perfection and theosis.

Remember, God, as Holy Trinity, is made of three Persons: Father, Son and Holy Spirit. Know that they are real living Persons. In Eastern Orthodox Christianity, prayers have been formulated for each Person. God is a Living Being and – whether we call on the Father, Son or Holy Spirit – we must develop a relationship with God. Know that it is because of the Son, we know the Father. Here, you can see the uniqueness and beauty of the faith of the Christian people. No other religious people call on God as Father – as the Lord's Prayer expresses, "Our Father who art in heaven, Hallowed be thy name" (Matthew 6:9, RSV). Christians have an intimate love for the Godhead like no other religious people because of the Son. No other world religion teaches this intimate relationship with God. Developing a relationship with God as Father is beautiful, comforting and filled with love.

Just as with every important relationship, open honest communication is vital. And, we communicate to God through prayer. God knows everything – including our thoughts – and when we pray to God throughout the day, He hears us. We must speak with God through prayer to strengthen our relationship with Him. This will make us better and happier people.

Father Thomas Hopko explained that prayer is the "art of arts" and "science of sciences" that makes life livable and produces fruit through God's grace ("Foreword," viii). Unceasing prayer is not meant to remove the pain in life but is meant to help the praying person endure and embrace life's struggles as the only way to happiness in this fallen world on the way to Heaven. Bishop Ware identified the three levels of the Jesus Prayer. He explained,

> Normally three levels or degrees are distinguished in the saying of the Jesus Prayer. It starts as "prayer of the lips", oral prayer. Then it grows more inward, becoming "prayer of the intellect", mental prayer. Finally the intellect "descends" into the heart and is united with it, and so the prayer becomes "prayer of the heart" or, more exactly, "prayer of the intellect in the heart". At this level it becomes prayer of the whole person – no longer something that we think or say, but something that we are: for the ultimate purpose of the spiritual Way is not just a person who *says* prayers from time to time, but a person who *is* prayer all the time. The Jesus Prayer, that is to say, begins as a series of specific *acts* of prayer, but its eventual aim is to establish in the one who prays a *state* of prayer that is unceasing, which continues

uninterrupted even in the midst of other activities. (*The Orthodox Way*, 123)

Saint Ignatius said the Jesus Prayer "leads its practitioner from earth to heaven, and places him among the celestial inhabitants" (*On the Prayer of Jesus*, viii). When we pray the Jesus Prayer, we are among the angels.

When I was first learning the habit and developing the discipline of the Jesus Prayer, I used my prayer rope (in Greek, komboskini and in Russian, chotki) to help me repeat the prayer, and now, after many years of practice, the Jesus Prayer is always with me. In joy and in distress, the Jesus Prayer constantly springs like a geyser in my soul. It has become self-active and is always in me.

As Bishop Ware pointed out (*The Orthodox Church*, 297-299), the Jesus Prayer is effective and versatile. It can be used by anyone, at any time, in any place. The Jesus Prayer enters into the heart – meaning the Holy Spirit dwells in the person and the prayer recites itself spontaneously. The prayer is powerful because the power of God is in the Name of Jesus. It is the Divine Name. By praying to Jesus, we are invoking the Name of God. The Jesus Prayer is helpful at all types of moments – for reassurance and joy, while walking, during cold, when hungry, if ill or at harm, at home or in church. It is meant to be used during all aspects and with every activity in life.

Eventually, repeating the Jesus Prayer without ceasing will help one control wild imaginations and wandering thoughts and lead one to be fully aware of the divine presence. At first, this may not seem possible or, perhaps, overwhelming; but as the pilgrim showed and as I can attest, it will become delightfully natural and is a source of joy, strength and protection. Ultimately, we must pray unceasingly, so it is not only a part of us but is us. Human beings are meant to be prayerful creatures. It is to our benefit to pray the Jesus Prayer without ceasing, so we can reach our fullest divine potential.

I have learned so much from books – which is a big reason for why I write. It is my natural inclination to share in writing what I have learned. In my life, there have been great men and women of Christian literature who have taught me much. I am in their debt and I pray they are or will be in Heaven with God where I hope to join them. This exposition has been catalyzed and made possible foremost by *The Way of a Pilgrim*'s anonymous author and has also been made possible by the writings of Saint Ignatius Brianchaninov, Father Thomas Hopko and Bishop Kallistos (Timothy) Ware as well as translators R.M. French and Olga Savin. The specific literature written by them that has helped me has been documented in the Bibliography and Works Cited section of this exposition. I thank God for them and may their writings lead generations into eternal life.

The Way of a Pilgrim Analysis

First Narrative

The Way of a Pilgrim is part story and part instruction manual on prayer, and the First Narrative is a great introductory chapter. The pilgrim confessed to us that he is a Christian, a great sinner and a homeless wanderer. His only worldly belongings were a knapsack, dried bread and the Holy Bible.

At church, the pilgrim was struck by the words of Saint Paul who said, "Pray without ceasing" (1 Thessalonians 5:17, KJV). With these words, the pilgrim's story takes off. This is reminiscent of Saint Antony the Great's story when he was in church and was struck by the words of Jesus Christ who said, "If you would be perfect, go, sell what you possess and give to the poor, and you will have treasure in heaven; and come, follow me" (Matthew 19:21, RSV). These words set Antony on a life changing journey, and the words of Saint Paul did the same for the pilgrim. Praying without ceasing is the thesis and main point of the story. We discover how it is possible to pray without ceasing.

The pilgrim's first step to find out how to pray without ceasing was to visit churches and preachers. However, his first step was unfruitful. He learned nothing on how to succeed in prayer. His next step was to seek a guide. His first guide in how to pray without ceasing was a landowner. The landowner gave the pilgrim a description but not an explanation. When he visited the abbot at a monastery, the abbot showed him a page in a spiritual book, which gave him an excellent clue about unceasing prayer. The book said that to pray without ceasing is the prayer of the mind. From this piece of information, the pilgrim questioned how the mind can pray without being distracted. The abbot did not give him a full explanation, but as the pilgrim continued his journey, he found answers.

Then, a starets (Russian term for spiritual elder) provided the pilgrim with encouraging words telling him that his longing to acquire unceasing interior prayer was the calling of God. According to the starets, the problem in the way most preachers teach about prayer is that they are scholastic instead of mystical. He explained,

> Many people reason quite the wrong way round about prayer, thinking that good actions and all sorts of preliminary measures render us capable of prayer. But quite the reverse is the case; it is prayer which bears fruit in good works and all the virtues. Those who reason so take, incorrectly, the fruits and the results of prayer for the means of attaining it, and this

is to depreciate the power of prayer. (R.M. French, 6)

The starets explained further that…

> the Apostle Paul says, 'I exhort therefore that first of all supplications be made' (1 Tim. 2:1). The first thing laid down in the Apostle's words about prayer is that the work of prayer comes before everything else: 'I exhort therefore that first of all. 'The Christian is bound to perform many good works, but before all else what he ought to do is to pray, for without prayer no other good work whatever can be accomplished. Without prayer he can not find the way to the Lord, he cannot understand the truth, he cannot crucify the flesh with its passions and lusts, his heart cannot be enlightened with the light of Christ, he cannot be savingly united to God. None of [9] those things can be effected unless they are preceded by constant prayer… [It] is the mother of all spiritual blessings. 'Capture the mother, and she will bring you the children,' said St. Isaac the Syrian. Learn first to acquire the power of prayer and you will easily practice all the other virtues. (R.M. French, 6)

The starets pointed out that Apostle Paul said, 'For we know not what we should pray for as we ought'

(Romans 8:26, KJV), but within our abilities is the frequency and regularity of our prayer. The key prayer for praying unceasingly – without stopping – is the Jesus Prayer. In the following passage from the text, the starets introduced the Jesus Prayer. He explained,

> The continuous interior prayer of Jesus is a constant uninterrupted calling upon the divine name of Jesus with the lips, in the spirit, in the heart, while forming a mental picture of His constant presence, and imploring His grace, during every occupation, at all times, in all places, even during sleep. The appeal is couched in these terms, 'Lord Jesus Christ, have mercy on me.' One who accustoms himself to this appeal experiences as a result so deep a consolation and so great a need to offer [10] the prayer always that he can no longer live without it, and it will continue to voice itself within him of its own accord. (R.M. French, 6)

The starets explained that we can learn about the prayer in the *Philokalia*. In it are the teachings of unceasing interior prayer by twenty-five holy Fathers. It is lofty in wisdom, though not holier than the Bible. It "contains clear explanations of what the Bible holds in secret" (R.M. French, 6). Holy Scripture "is a dazzling sun, and this book, the

Philokalia, is the piece of glass which we use to enable us to contemplate the sun in its imperial splendor" (R.M. French, 6). In Greek, philokalia means love of the good, the beautiful.

To begin to practice unceasing interior prayer, a person should sit alone and in silence, shut his eyes, look with his mind into his heart, and as he breathes, repeat: "Lord Jesus Christ, have mercy on me." He should also strive to banish all thoughts. To fully live a proper inner spiritual life, a person must have a priest or monk as a spiritual director for guidance.

In order to visit the starets for guidance, the pilgrim worked for a peasant by guarding his kitchen garden for the summer. The pilgrim lived alone near the garden in a hut, which was peaceful lodging to learn interior prayer. From time to time, he visited the starets.

After a week of learning unceasing prayer, a great inner heaviness emerged. The starets explained that was the kingdom of darkness waging war against him and that the pilgrim's humility needed to be tested, which meant it was too soon to enter the deepest heart. To overcome the obstacle the pilgrim faced during inner prayer, the starets taught him that the holy Fathers prescribed to banish all thoughts. Repeat: "Lord Jesus Christ, have mercy on me!" A person must compel himself always to repeat this. The starets explained that this would open the doors of the heart. The starets taught him to repeat the Jesus Prayer as often as possible and to begin – with the chotki (Russian term for prayer rope) – repeating the prayer three thousand times a day – whether standing, sitting, walking or lying down. He must not be loud or rush. God will help. This advice helped me when I began to learn the prayer. A chotki (prayer rope) is called a komboskini in Greek, and it is typically made of wool and comes in different lengths. The one I used to practice the Jesus Prayer had thirty-three knots for Jesus's age when he died as traditionally honored by the Church, and I wore it around my wrist.

When he applied the starets's advice to his prayer, the pilgrim, for two days, encountered some difficulty. Then, it became easier, and if he stopped, he experienced a compelling need to recite the prayer, again. Soon, he prayed with comfort and ease without exerting force. Then, the starets doubled to six thousand the number of times to repeat the prayer in full faith and told him that God would bestow His mercy on him. The pilgrim practiced the Jesus Prayer in strict solitude and focus for one week with no disturbance or other activity. The result was that when he stopped praying, he felt as though something were missing. Within a week, he became accustomed to the prayer.

The starets was like a doctor giving a prescription to the pilgrim. The pilgrim told the starets his inner condition, and the starets diagnosed that the pilgrim became accustomed to the prayer and that he should strengthen this habit. Now, the starets prescribed the pilgrim to repeat the prayer twelve thousand times a day, remain in solitude and visit him every two weeks for counsel.

The pilgrim was not a typical patient or student. And, he was not a man working a 9AM-5PM office job in New York City. He was a wandering ascetic who was not fully integrated in society and lived a lot like a monk. He was not exactly a hermit like Saint Antony – the Father of Monasticism – but like Antony, he cherished discipline and prayer. Most of us do not live like him, but we can learn from him the importance and power of prayer.

The pilgrim acquired physical bodily pains from praying so much. He became weary, his tongue became numb, his jaw felt stiff, he had pain in his mouth, and he had pain in his thumb from counting on the chotki. Also, his wrist felt inflamed up to his elbow though this was pleasant, which compelled him to pray more. The habit of prayer became stronger and more pleasant, so he became more willing to practice it.

The Jesus Prayer took on a second nature type quality within the pilgrim. It was awakened in him. As if with a mind of its own, his desire strove toward reciting the Jesus Prayer. He was filled with light and joy as his tongue and mouth spoke the words on their own without any effort. He was filled with such joy that he felt as if he were on another planet. He continued to call on the name of Jesus Christ with great ease feeling drawn to it. The pilgrim explained his experience to his starets who said,

> "Be thankful to God that this desire for the prayer and this facility in it have been manifested in you. It is a natural consequence which follows constant effort and spiritual achievement. So a machine to the principal wheel of which one gives a drive works for a long while afterward by itself, but if it is to go on working still longer, one must oil it and give it another drive. Now you see with what admirable gifts God in His love for mankind has endowed even the bodily nature of man. You see what feelings can be produced even outside a state of grace in a soul which is sinful and with passions unsubdued, as you yourself have experienced. But how wonderful, how delightful, and how consoling a thing it is when God is pleased to grant the gift of self-acting spiritual prayer, and to cleanse the soul from all sensuality! It is a condition which is impossible to describe, and the discovery of this mystery of prayer is a foretaste on earth of the bliss of heaven. Such happiness is reserved for those who seek after God in the simplicity of a loving heart. Now I give you my permission to say your prayer as often as you wish and as often as you can. Try to devote every moment you are awake to the

> prayer, call on the name of Jesus Christ without [16] counting the number of times, and submit yourself humbly to the will of God, looking to Him for help. I am sure He will not forsake you and that He will lead you into the right path." (R.M. French, 8)

This was the natural reward of the pilgrim's labor. It started as a habit through much repetition, and then God blessed the pilgrim with the gifts of peace and joy. As the starets said, "the discovery of this mystery of prayer is a foretaste on earth of the bliss of heaven" and that it is given only to those who earnestly seek and love God (R.M. French, 8). The starets prescribed that the pilgrim's final step was to devote every waking moment to prayer – but no more counting – and to submit humbly to God and await His help. The pilgrim spent his entire summer repeating the Jesus Prayer. He even dreamed that he was reciting the Jesus Prayer. All the people he encountered appeared very dear to him. Thoughts seemed to vanish – the only thing that he thought of was prayer – and his heart felt a warmth. Church no longer felt tiring as it once had, and his solitary hut seemed like a magnificent palace.

    I can confirm the authenticity of the pilgrim's experience with the Jesus Prayer. This is exactly what happened to me but over a much longer time. Living in a metropolitan area in the United States of America and while working in society, I reached this level of prayer in more than months and more like a year or two years.

At the end of the summer, the starets died. The one possession from the starets that the pilgrim asked for was his starets's chotki. After the pilgrim was released from his job, he had nowhere to live, and once again set off wandering, but he was not worried because he possessed the Jesus Prayer. Calling on Jesus Christ with joy, everyone he met seemed dear to him. With the money he earned from his kitchen garden job, the pilgrim bought a copy of the *Philokalia*. The pilgrim felt the Jesus Prayer to be more precious and sweeter than anything else in the world. He treasured and enjoyed the upliftment of the Jesus Prayer as he walked (even during stretches of over forty-seven miles), in bitter cold, in hunger, when feeling ill, in pain, if someone offended him. He had no vain cares that concern this world and longed only for solitude. His only desire was to pray unceasingly because of the joy it brought him.

At this point, the pilgrim had not yet learned the prayer of the inner heart, but he had met his first goal and understood Apostle Paul's words to – "Pray without ceasing."

Second Narrative

The pilgrim began the Second Narrative by telling us that he wandered for a long time. Finally, he decided to look for solitude so he could study the *Philokalia* and decided to head for Siberia.

As the pilgrim prayed the Jesus Prayer, he found that the prayer began to move of its own accord from his lips into his heart, and he began to listen attentively to the words of his heart. As he prayed the Jesus Prayer, his love for Jesus Christ grew, and he wanted to embrace His feet and thank Him with tears for His love and grace in allowing him – an unworthy and sinful creature – to find so great a consolation in His Name. The pilgrim experienced a warmth in his heart, and so he read the *Philokalia* to verify that the experience was not delusion or pride.

His starets had died, but they continued to have contact in dreams. There, his starets reminded him of the importance of humility.

As he was traveling, the pilgrim was clobbered and robbed. He burst into tears – more than any other reason – because his books – his Bible and his *Philokalia* – were gone. After this catastrophe, his starets appeared to him, again, in a dream, and his starets provided him with wisdom telling him to learn detachment from earthly material possessions which will ease the journey to Heaven. God wants the denial of will, desires and attachments, so the Christian is totally submitted to His Divine Will. Quoting Apostle Paul, the starets told him that God desires all men to be saved (1 Timothy 2:3b), and so with the temptation, God will also provide the way of escape (1 Corinthians 10:13). At these words, the pilgrim woke up and felt a new strength, and his soul was filled with light and peace.

Then, a curious circumstance unfolded to the pilgrim's good fortune. He caught up with a convoy of convicts that included the two men who robbed him, and the pilgrim was reunited with his books. As a result of this run in, he made a friend with the captain who had read the Bible. When he was in the army, the captain struggled with alcoholism. A monk unexpectedly came to the aid of the captain. Reminded of his brother, the monk suggested to the captain that when he felt the urge to drink, he should, rather, read the Bible. The monk recommended reading the Bible because alcoholic addiction is the work of the devil and the words of God Himself frighten the spirits of darkness. According to the monk, if you do not understand what you are reading in the Bible, you should keep on reading diligently. And so, the captain continued and read another chapter, and he began to understand. Reading the Bible helped the captain resist and develop an aversion to alcohol. He had been free of alcohol for exactly twenty years, and he was transformed and blessed with a new life. The captain made sure to read one Gospel from the Bible every day.

The captain's story of being healed by God, Jesus and the Bible is not unique. The story reminded the pilgrim of a craftsman he knew who would repeat the Jesus Prayer thirty-three times whenever he felt the urge to drink. In this way, the craftsman reached sobriety, and three years later, he entered a monastery. When the captain asked the pilgrim, which is the best – the prayer of Jesus or the Gospels – the pilgrim gave him a powerful answer and told him,

> "It's all one and the same thing… What the Gospel is, that the prayer of Jesus is also,' for the Divine Name of Jesus Christ holds in itself the whole [28] gospel truth. The holy Fathers say that the prayer of Jesus is a summary of the Gospels." (R.M. French, 12)

When reading the *Philokalia* for the first time after it was stolen, the pilgrim was filled with joy – as if he were reunited after a long separation with his father or with a friend who had resurrected from the dead. He covered the book with kisses and thanked God.

The pilgrim was surprised to read in the *Philokalia* that a man could perform three different activities simultaneously – for example, a monk can eat in the refectory, listen to the daily reading and pray within himself… all at the same time. A mystery was revealed to him that the mind and heart are separate entities.

After parting ways with the captain and setting off, again, on his journey, the pilgrim backtracked to give a ruble that he promised to the criminals who robbed him. He debated within himself whether to give them the rubble or not. He thought "No" because they beat and robbed him and were under arrest; and he thought "Yes" because the Bible teaches to feed your enemy and Jesus said to love your enemies. Reading this, we can reflect on what we would do if we were in the pilgrim's position. The pilgrim showed love for his enemy and said something remarkable and deep to them. He said, "Repent and pray! Jesus Christ loves men; he will not forsake you" (R.M. French, 12). And, with that, he left them and went on his way.

    I hope my audience can see how the pilgrim developed a love for reading as well as see the true value and power of reading. No one should ever think that reading is boring or for the weak, that it is only academic and not practical. Reading is a highly valuable skill to enhance one's life. It can make you a better version of yourself. Reading is the most thorough and comprehensive way to learn, and learning is always fun! Learning is the reward of reading. I discovered this as a young man, and I trained myself to read, and I loved how much I was learning. The pilgrim was a perfect example of the power in reading – not as entertainment, rather for knowledge. He explained,

> After doing some thirty miles along the main road I thought I would take a bypath so that I might be more by myself and read more quietly. For a long while I walked through the

> heart of the forest, and but rarely came upon a village. At times I passed almost the whole day sitting under the trees and carefully reading the *Philokalia*, from which I gained a surprising amount of knowledge. My heart kindled with desire for union with God by means of interior prayer, and I was eager to learn it under the guidance and control of my book. At the same time I felt sad that I had no dwelling where I could give myself up quietly to reading all the while. (R.M. French, 12-13)

The pilgrim developed a deeper passion for God through reading the *Philokalia*. He understood the Church Fathers when they said the *Philokalia* is the key to unlocking the mysteries of Holy Scripture. The pilgrim's view of God's Creation was transformed from reading the *Philokalia* and from praying with his heart. In the natural terrain, he was filled with delight. All "things [in Creation] prayed to God and sang His praise" (R.M. French, 13).

After journeying for a long time, the pilgrim found himself in uninhabited land with no more dried bread. Then, a dog popped up out of the woods. This helped the pilgrim because it led him to a peasant, and they struck up a friendly conversation. The pilgrim said he was envious of the peasant and his mud hut. Would you be envious to want to live as the peasant in a mud hut? The peasant had been eating only bread for ten years, and the only thing he drank was water. As a result of meeting the peasant, the pilgrim had a place to stay. He had peace and solitude to read the *Philokalia*. He was overjoyed and thanked God for His mercy. A book like this should prompt us to ask – what do we really need in life and what will truly make us happy?

The peasant was a simple man who once led a prosperous life – although, not sinless. He cheated and cursed, but he changed his ways because of an old deacon who would read aloud from an extremely old book about the Last Judgement for pay. One time, the peasant listened and got scared and decided to change.

The peasant had been living in his mud hut for ten years and ate once a day. He lived a solitary holy life in the forest. However, he said lately he found himself attacked by thoughts and doubts about the life he chose. His mind was hounded with thoughts – such as if sins can really be prayed away, if there will really be a resurrection, if there really is a hell. He contemplated how life is hard and that we should just enjoy ourselves. The pilgrim sympathized with the peasant's distress. He saw how the powers of darkness impact everyone and that a person must strengthen himself with the Word of God against the spiritual enemy. The pilgrim tried to help by reading the *Philokalia* to him:

> So with the object of helping this brother and doing all I could to strengthen his faith, I took

the *Philokalia* out of my knapsack. Turning to the 109th chapter of Isaiah the Solitary, I read it to him. I set out to prove to him the uselessness and vanity of avoiding sin merely from fear of the tortures of hell. I told him that the soul could be freed from sinful thoughts only by guarding the mind and [34] cleansing the heart, and that this could be done by interior prayer. I added that according to the holy Fathers, one who performs saving works simply from the fear of hell follows the way of bondage, and he who does the same just in order to be rewarded with the kingdom of heaven follows the path of a bargainer with God. The one they call a slave, the other a hireling. But God wants us to come to Him as sons to their Father; He wants us to behave ourselves honorably from love for Him and zeal for His service; He wants us to find our happiness in uniting ourselves with Him in a saving union of mind and heart. "However much you spend yourself on treating your body hardly," I said, "you will never find peace of mind that way, and unless you have God in your mind and the ceaseless prayer of Jesus in your heart, you will always be likely to fall back into sin for the very slightest reason. Set to work, my brother, upon the ceaseless saying of the prayer of Jesus. You have such a good chance of doing so here in this lonely place, and in a short while you will see the gain of it. No godless thoughts will then be able to get at you, and the true faith and love for Jesus Christ will be shown to you. You will then understand how the dead will be raised, and you will see the Last judgment in its true light. The prayer will make you feel such lightness and such bliss in your heart that you will be astonished at it yourself, and your wholesome way of life will be neither dull nor troublesome to you." (R.M. French, 14)

The pilgrim was happy because the cave provided him with peace and quiet to read the *Philokalia* and learn the unceasing self-acting prayer of the heart. To help him with his difficulty in understanding all of the *Philokalia*, the pilgrim prayed to the Lord, and then his departed starets appeared to him in a dream and explained the *Philokalia*. The starets told him that he should not read according to the order printed in the book and that the work of these Fathers contains the complete instruction on interior prayer of the heart that is accessible to all. Then, a remarkable and supernatural action happened in the dream. His departed starets directed him on which passages to read in the *Philokalia* by highlighting them with a piece of charcoal. When he woke up, the pilgrim found the highlights that were marked during the dream to be in his *Philokalia*. The pilgrim was astonished, and this made him sure of the truth of his dream and that his revered master of blessed memory was pleasing to God.

After reading the *Philokalia* in the starets's order, the pilgrim felt his soul burned with desire and eagerness to experience personally all that he read. This book – *The Way of a Pilgrim* – is like a long introduction to and key highlights of the Jesus Prayer in the *Philokalia*. With the Jesus Prayer, the pilgrim incorporated methods and techniques with his heart. He explained,

> So I began by searching out my heart in the way Simeon the new theologian teaches. With my eyes shut I gazed in thought, that is, in imagination, upon my heart. I tried to picture it there in the left side of my breast and to listen carefully to its beating. I started doing this several times a day, for half an hour at a time, and at first I felt nothing but a sense of darkness. But little by little after a fairly short time I was able to picture my heart and to note its movement, and further with the help of my breathing I could put into it and draw from it the prayer of Jesus in the manner taught by the saints, Gregory of Sinai, Callistus, and Ignatius. When drawing the air in I looked in spirit into my heart and said, "Lord Jesus Christ," and when breathing out again, I said,

> "Have [38] mercy on me." I did this at first for an hour at a time, then for two hours, then for as long as I could, and in the end almost all day long. If any difficulty arose, if sloth or doubt came upon me, I hastened to take up the *Philokalia* and read again those parts which dealt with the work of the heart, and then once more I felt ardor and zeal for the prayer. (R.M. French, 15)

Then, the pilgrim experienced different sensations in his heart and mind from praying to Jesus in his heart. He explained,

> When about three weeks had passed I felt a pain in my heart, and then a most delightful warmth, as well as consolation and peace. This aroused me still more and spurred me on more and more to give great care to the saying of the prayer so that all my thoughts were taken up with it and I felt a very great joy. From this time I began to have from time to time a number of different feelings in my heart and mind. Sometimes my heart would feel as though it were bubbling with joy; such lightness, freedom, and consolation were in it. Sometimes I felt a burning love for Jesus Christ and for all God's creatures. Sometimes my eyes brimmed over with tears of thankfulness to God, who was so merciful to

> me, a wretched sinner. Sometimes my understanding, which had been so stupid before, was given so much light that I could easily grasp and dwell upon matters of which up to now I had not been able even to think at all. Sometimes that sense of a warm gladness in my heart spread throughout my whole being and I was deeply moved as the fact of the presence of God everywhere was brought home to me. Sometimes by calling upon the name of Jesus I was overwhelmed with bliss, and now I knew the meaning of the words "The kingdom of God is within you" [Luke 17:21]. (R.M. French, 15-16)

The effects of the prayer of the heart manifested in three ways: in the spirit, in the feelings, through revelations.

The pilgrim was in solitude with his prayerful exercise for five months – these are extraordinary circumstances and not typical for a person living within society. As a result, the prayer did not cease and his soul was filled with gratitude to the Lord, while his heart languished in unceasing joy. The prayer of the heart matured within the pilgrim. He explained,

> For a very long while I wandered about in different places until I reached Irkutsk. The self-acting prayer in my heart was a comfort

and consolation all the way; whatever I met with it never ceased to gladden me, though it did so to different degrees at different times. Wherever I was, whatever I did or gave myself up to, it never hindered things, nor was hindered by them. If I am working at anything the prayer goes on by itself in my heart, [40] and the work gets on faster. If I am listening carefully to anything, or reading, the prayer never stops; at one and the same time I am aware of both just as if I were made into two people, or as if there were two souls in my one body. Lord! what a mysterious thing man is! "How manifold are thy works, O Lord! In wisdom hast thou made them all" [Psalm 104:24]. (R.M. French, 16)

Next, the pilgrim wrote about one example of a remarkable experience during his journey that concerned his starets's chotki. The pilgrim was attacked by a wolf, and his chotki became entangled around the wolf's neck and was caught on the branch of a dead tree. The pilgrim made the sign of the Cross over himself, approached to grab the chotki, and then the wolf broke loose and took off without a trace.

A bit later, the pilgrim encountered two men at the village inn: an old man who was a teacher in the public school and a fat middle aged man who was a clerk of the county court. Both were upper-crust people. The clerk made a joke about the pilgrim's broken chotki and laughed after the pilgrim told the story about the wolf. The clerk said miracles are for holy frauds. Then, the teacher responded by defending the pilgrim and explaining the sensible and spiritual nature of the pilgrim's story. The pilgrim was pleased with the way the teacher spoke and so told him about his starets. The clerk grumbled that a person can lose his mind reading the Bible too much. The pilgrim told the teacher the story about his starets, the *Philokalia* and the charcoal markings. The teacher provided his answer for the mystery, then sharply changed the conversation to see what the book is about. Then, the teacher told the pilgrim his views on interior prayer. The two men that the pilgrim encountered were very different, but both left an impression on the pilgrim as we see in the book. They had strong dynamic personalities. The teacher was compassionate but a bit of a know-it-all – some information he provided was correct, some was incorrect. The clerk was a jokester and a bit bitter with life and enjoyed drinking.

    The next person the pilgrim wrote about meeting on his journey was a priest. The pilgrim was hired to keep an eye on the workers who were building the new stone church and to sit in the chapel accepting donations for the new building. A young peasant girl visited the chapel frequently to pray. The pilgrim advised her to pray the Lord's Prayer, the "Rejoice O Virgin Theotokos" and the Jesus Prayer.

The girl took his advice and was drawn to reciting the Jesus Prayer continuously and was filled with gladness. The pilgrim became popular, and many visited just to see him. We learn that the young girl faced a problem. Her father decided to marry her off, and so she wanted to run away. The pilgrim advised the young girl to pray to God more earnestly about this.

The pilgrim wanted to leave his work in the chapel for quiet surroundings to pray. He had too many harmful distractions where he was in his current situation. The priest and the pilgrim had different views about his role in the community and how to live a holy life serving God. Both provided strong and persuasive arguments. The priest said the pilgrim could pray where he was, his bread was provided, his good presence was profitable for God's Church and it was more pleasing to God than solitude. The priest believed it is better to be with the community to benefit it. The pilgrim said there are many types of people in the Church, including hermits. Each has his own unique calling and his own path to Salvation. Many saints gave up ecclesiastical offices and fled to the desert's solitude because of too many distractions and temptations in society. The pilgrim believed if the saints needed to protect themselves from mingling with people, then what must a poor sinner like him resort to.

Next, the young girl who was praying ran into the pilgrim. She was set for her betrothal and asked the pilgrim to take her to some women's monastery. The pilgrim felt he was unable to help, but he suggested she pray to God, and if she did not want to get married, then she could make up some illness as an excuse. The pilgrim explained this is called pretending for the sake of Salvation and that there were holy female saints who had done the same. Then, four peasants grabbed the girl and forcibly brought the pilgrim to jail for seducing the girl. The priest arrived to help by testifying on the pilgrim's behalf. The magistrate concluded that the girl would go back to her father and the pilgrim be kicked out of town. The pilgrim left in good spirits. He explained,

> So saying, he [the magistrate] got down from the table and went off to bed, while I was taken back to jail. Early in the morning two country policemen came, flogged me, and drove me out of the village. I went off thanking God that He counted me worthy to suffer for His name. This comforted me and gave still more warmth and glow to my ceaseless interior prayer. None of these things made me feel at all cast down. It was as though they happened to someone else and I merely watched them. Even the flogging was within my power to bear. The prayer brought sweetness into my heart and made me unaware, so to speak, of everything else. (R.M. French, 19)

The pilgrim bumped into the young girl's mother who told him some good news for the young girl that the bridegroom backed off from marriage because the girl ran away from him.

The pilgrim continued his journey, found a couple of haystacks and fell asleep. In a dream, his starets visited him. The starets told him that life is not easy, that the best sometimes face disgrace for the spiritual benefit of others and that those who pray most earnestly are attacked by the most terrible temptations. In the dream, the starets explained that great men gave their lives over to unceasing prayer and that with their knowledge, their next step was to teach this prayer to others and to awaken in all people a desire to pray unceasingly.

The pilgrim's next incident during his journey began with his irresistible desire to receive Holy Communion on the Annunciation of the Most Pure Theotokos when the Church commemorates Archangel Gabriel's announcement to the Virgin Mary that she would give birth to Jesus – the Incarnation of God. However, the pilgrim was confronted with bad weather – snow, rain, wind, cold. He fell into a creek and became soaking wet. This obstacle manifested into a big problem when he developed pain in his legs, which remained wet, and then his legs became completely paralyzed. On the third day, he was kicked out from his lodging and lay on the church steps for about another two days. A peasant approached him and offered to cure him. They agreed that if the peasant cured him, then the pilgrim would pay back the peasant by teaching the peasant's son how to write.

And so, the peasant set about to cure him. With a bushel of rotting bones, the peasant created a tar that became a reddish oily liquid that smelled like raw meat. The pilgrim rubbed this liquid into his legs five times a day. By the end of the week, the pilgrim's legs had recovered. He equated this miraculous healing with the wisdom of God's Creation – that decomposed bones can bring life to deadened limbs – and that this was a pledge of the resurrection.

The pilgrim taught the boy how to write by writing out the Jesus Prayer, instead of using a grammar book. We also learn that the pilgrim had a physical disability – a disabled arm.

The curious steward – who the boy was an apprentice for – discovered that the pilgrim studied the *Philokalia*. The steward had disregard for the *Philokalia* as very strange magic similar to that of India and Bukhara's fanatics and considered it stupidity. He believed in praying simply in the morning the Our Father (the Lord's Prayer) and not this endless repetition that can take you out of your mind and hurt your heart. The pilgrim listened but was not offended by the curious steward's words. The pilgrim calmly corrected him and called him Batyushka, which is a Russian term that means Little

Father, a term of respect and affection. The pilgrim defended the *Philokalia* by explaining that it was not written by ordinary Greek monks but by the greatest and holiest men of long ago. The monks of India and Bukhara adopted and ruined it. The *Philokalia* is rooted in the Holy Bible. The pilgrim provided support from the Bible and the saints. The steward replied that those teachings do not apply to ordinary people who live in the world. According to the pilgrim and the *Philokalia's* holy Fathers, that is not true. Even good people, living in the world, managed to learn unceasing prayer. Many parts of *The Way of a Pilgrim* are apologetic literature that defend the Jesus Prayer and the *Philokalia*. The steward was impressed and wanted to borrow the pilgrim's *Philokalia*. Instead, the pilgrim copied out the passage he read to give to the steward.

After the pilgrim – out of love – copied the *Philokalia* passage for the steward, the steward invited the pilgrim to his home to read from the book to him and his wife. One time, when the pilgrim visited, they all had dinner and the steward's wife choked on a fish bone. In a dream, the starets visited the pilgrim to guide him in how to help the old lady. Because the old lady had an aversion to lamp oil, a spoonful would induce vomiting which would cure her.

After the cure of the wife, word spread quickly that the pilgrim was a visionary, healer and witch doctor. People came to him and treated him with great respect. After a week, the pilgrim left because he was afraid of vainglory. This is just like Saint Antony the Great – the Father of Monasticism – who departed further into the Egyptian desert to avoid vainglory.

Once again embarking on his solitary journey, the pilgrim felt that the prayer increasingly comforted him, and his heart bubbled over with boundless love for Jesus Christ. The pilgrim felt the solitude during his journey consoled him. When he reached the city of Irkutsk and venerated the relics of Saint Innocent, he met a local merchant. They spoke and the pilgrim told him about his travels. The merchant recommended the pilgrim travel to old Jerusalem and that he would help by arranging and paying for the pilgrim's journey. The pilgrim was overcome with joy and gratitude and thanked God.

Before the pilgrim met the local merchant, he began to wonder where he should go next. He reached his destination and was totally free with no responsibility other than to survive and pray. The pilgrim is unique. We might ask ourselves if we would like to live like him with all the freedom in the world to pray but also with the adversity and uncertainty of being a homeless wanderer. Nonetheless, we can and should learn from him and his experiences with the Jesus Prayer.

Third Narrative

Before leaving the city, the pilgrim visited his spiritual father who blessed him and who asked the pilgrim to talk about his life before he became a pilgrim. The Third Narrative is the pilgrim's autobiography.

The pilgrim's parents died when he was two. He and his older brother were raised by his grandfather who was prosperous, honest and kept an inn. The pilgrim recounted how his arm became disabled. His older brother drank heavily and when the pilgrim was seven, they were lying on the stove; his brother pushed him off, he hurt his left arm, and it withered up. His grandfather realized he would not be able to work the land, so he taught him how to read and write by copying the Bible. Once the pilgrim learned to read and write, his grandfather told him that God revealed reading and writing to him which would make a man out of him and that he must thank the Lord and pray more in church and at home.

When the pilgrim was seventeen years old, his grandmother died, and his grandfather arranged that he marry a twenty-year-old girl. Then, as the grandfather was dying, he left his grandson – the pilgrim – with the following parting words,

> 'I leave you my house and all I have. Obey your conscience, deceive no one, and above all pray to God; everything comes from Him. Trust [62] in Him only. Go to church

regularly, read your Bible, and remember me and your grandmother in your prayers. Here is my money, that also I give you; there is a thousand rubles. Take care of it. Do not waste it, but do not be miserly either; give some of it to the poor and to God's church.' (R.M. French, 23-24)

After this, the grandfather died, and the pilgrim buried him. The brother was jealous of the pilgrim, and the brother plotted to kill him, stole his money and set fire to the hut and inn. However, the pilgrim was grateful that he was able to save the Bible. The brother disappeared and boasted about the stealing and fire. The pilgrim and his wife lived in a small cabin as landless peasants. The wife worked as a seamstress, and the pilgrim would read the Bible to her. She would cry because of the Bible's beautiful words. They fasted, did prostrations and lived peacefully for two years. They prayed with great delight.

After two years, the wife became ill, received her last Communion and died. This changed the pilgrim's life. He started wandering and begging. Filled with grief over losing his wife, he sold his hut, gained a permanent disability passport and took his Bible and set off. He had been journeying for thirteen years. First, he journeyed to Kiev to visit the relics of God's worthy saints and ask for their intercession. He saw many churches and monasteries. But, he explained that more recently, he traveled by the fields. Next was Jerusalem. The pilgrim was thirty-three years old when he told his spiritual father about his life. That age is significant because it is the age of Jesus Christ at His death.

Fourth Narrative

    The pilgrim reaffirmed to his spiritual father the truth of the proverb, "Man proposes, but God disposes" (a proverb crystalized in Thomas à Kempis's *The Imitation of Christ*). This means man makes plans, but God decides their success or failure. So, we must remain humble and submit to God and His Will. We must trust in Him. He is Almighty. The older I get, the more I realize the truth of this proverb. Life is mysterious; however, we should have reassurance that if our wills are aligned with God's Will, we will prosper in whatever direction manifests.

    As the pilgrim was to begin his journey to Jerusalem, an unexpected incident popped up. A familiar man, who was once a pilgrim himself, knew of a traveling companion for the pilgrim for his trip to Jerusalem. The traveling companion was a local man, lower middle class, elderly and deaf; he hardly spoke, and with him was a horse and wagon. The familiar man explained the potential elderly traveling companion could use the pilgrim's assistance.

Because the elderly man was of an honest and decent family, the pilgrim agreed.

The pilgrim's spiritual father asked to hear more about the educational experiences the pilgrim encountered on his journeys. At this point in *The Way of a Pilgrim*, the storyline changes, again, and the remaining storyline is the pilgrim telling stories within the narrative.

The pilgrim explained he did not remember all the experiences and events of his journeys because so many things, both good and bad, happened to him that he could not remember them all. Plus, his attention was always more focused on prayer – and to forget the past and strive ahead, as Apostle Paul taught (Philippians 3:13-14). Even his late starets advised him to control his memories and thoughts. His starets told him that the enemy lures us away from prayer because the enemy finds prayer unbearable. The enemy causes the soul to scorn converse with God. The starets said prayer must significantly exceed even the time spent on any other pious activity.

The pilgrim recalled a memory ingrained in his mind. It began with some good people in a city. These good people provided him with fresh bread, a sturdy knapsack and salt. As he continued his journey, he entered a poor village with a wooden church and encountered two extremely well-dressed children, aged five or six, who told the pilgrim to follow them to their mother who loved the poor.

After the mother welcomed the pilgrim, the pilgrim called her affectionate greeting more precious than her offer of refreshments. He said he would pray God blesses her for her biblical love of pilgrims. The prayer was kindled in his heart and he wanted peace and solitude to pray. Planning to leave, he called her Matushka, which is a Russian term that means Little Mother. However, the woman did not accept his decision. She wanted him to stay and meet her husband, the judge, and pray the Liturgy with them the following day on Sunday. Then, they had dinner together.

The woman was a descendant of a significant historical figure. Her mother was the great-granddaughter of Saint Joasaph of Belgorod. The woman and her now husband had a unique relationship. He was an orphaned young man who grew up with her family in their house. After wedding the couple and settling her estate on them, the woman's mother entered a monastery and became a nun. Heeding her mother's instructions to live a Christian life, the woman and her husband provided a unique living situation with a guesthouse for the poor, which included ten crippled and needy people.

When the husband returned home, he and the pilgrim entered his study, which had many books and magnificent icons, including a life size figure of Christ on a crucifix. The pilgrim called it God's paradise with Christ, His Most Pure Mother and His holy saints. The master loved to read and had many spiritual books in his library. He loved to read about prayer. When the wife was reading aloud, the pilgrim simultaneously prayed in his heart. Then, he felt as if his starets's spirit had penetrated his own spirit and illuminated it. After the reading, they discussed what they read.

The pilgrim considered the Lord's Prayer (the Our Father) to be more exalted and more precious than all other recorded Christian prayers because it was given to us by the Lord Jesus Christ Himself. The holy Fathers of the *Philokalia* approached the Lord's Prayer through a contemplative and mystical lens. Through this lens, we see that...

- "Our Father, Who art in heaven" means that God is the heavenly Father and that we are to remember our obligation to live in His presence.
- "hallowed be Thy Name" is a direct request for the interior prayer of the heart, a request that the most holy Name of God be engraved upon the heart with self-acting prayer to sanctify our spirit.
- "Thy Kingdom come" means that we are praying for inner peace, tranquility and spiritual joy to come into our hearts.
- "give us this day our daily bread" means feeding the soul with heavenly bread – the Word of God – and uniting the soul with God

through remembering Him and through unceasing interior prayer of the heart.

In the pilgrim's tale, they do not finish analyzing the Lord's Prayer.

The husband said that it is almost impossible to attain interior prayer in the world. The pilgrim disagreed because God has admonished us all to do it. The Fathers offered us ways to attain and methods for the prayer of the heart – convenient methods that faithfully guide lay people. The pilgrim read a passage from the *Philokalia* that said calling upon the Name of God at all times in all places is more important than breathing, and it provided a practical method of praying without ceasing. The pilgrim said,

> 'If you would care to hear it, may I read you a little from the *Philokalia*?' I asked, taking up my copy. I found Peter the Damascene's article, part three, page 48, and read as follows: '"One must learn to call upon the name of God, more even than breathing-at all times, in all places, in every kind of occupation. The Apostle says, 'Pray without ceasing. 'That is, he teaches men to have the remembrance of God in all times and places and circumstances. If you are making something, you must call to mind the Creator of all things; if you see the light, remember the Giver of it; if you see the heavens and the

earth and the sea and all that is in them, wonder and praise the Maker of them. If you put on your clothes, recall Whose gift they are and thank Him Who provides for your life. In short, let every action be a cause of your remembering and praising God, and lo! you will be praying without ceasing and therein your soul will always rejoice." There, you see, this way of ceaseless prayer is simple and easy and within the reach of everybody so long as he has some amount of human feeling.' (R.M. French, 28)

Responding to the insightful reading, the husband was impressed and embraced the pilgrim with delight. He confessed he would order the *Philokalia* for himself, and he also copied the passage from the pilgrim.

The husband and wife gave the pilgrim extra special hospitality. After dinner and prayer, they brought the pilgrim a white shirt and socks, and he changed clothes. They changed his shoes as Christ washed the feet of His apostles. The pilgrim burst into tears, and they wept with him. The husband called the pilgrim a "fool for Christ." This is…

> A person who takes on an extreme form of asceticism in which even the appearance of sanity is abandoned and madness is feigned for the sake of Christ. "Holy fools" like this

were a fairly common sight in Russia right up until Soviet times and can even sometimes be seen today. The pilgrim was thought to be a fool for Christ by the landowner in the Fourth Narrative because he seemed too well educated to be a simple peasant. (Savin, Glossary)

The pilgrim said he did not acquire interior prayer on his own. It came to life in his heart through God's mercy and the guidance of his starets. The pilgrim said interior prayer is possible for anyone. The following is the method in brief:

> It costs nothing but the effort to sink down in silence into the depths of one's heart and call more and more upon the radiant name of Jesus. Everyone who does that feels at once the inward light, everything becomes understandable to him, he even catches sight in this light of some of the mysteries of the kingdom of God. (R.M. French, 29)

The pilgrim explained we have the ability to learn about the inner self, but people often choose aimless trifles of the world over the truth about the inner self. The pilgrim explained these two paths lead to stupidity or good judgement.

Two years before, the husband encountered an interesting man that prompted him to question if the pilgrim was a fool for Christ. This man was a wealthy prince, turned poor beggar. The husband and wife met this man when he came to them as an old and decrepit beggar. He became ill, and they nursed and cared for him. The day before he died, he wrote to his son his last will and testament with beautiful and excellent composition. This compelled the husband to ask him about his background and life. In society, he was a very wealthy prince, and he had committed an injustice when he was furious with his valet who he hit and who died. The prince was not bothered too much by this. As a result of his actions and disposition, he experienced tormenting apparitions – ghosts and visions – of hell. He explained,

> I regretted my rashness but soon forgot the' whole thing. Six weeks later, though, I began seeing the dead valet, in my dreams to begin with-every night he disturbed me and reproached me, incessantly repeating, 'Conscienceless man! You are my murderer!' As time went on, I began seeing him when I was awake also, wide awake. His appearances grew more and more frequent with the lapse of time, till the agitation he caused me became almost constant. And in the end he did not appear alone, but I saw at the same time other dead men whom I had treated very badly, and women whom I had seduced. They all

reproached me ceaselessly and gave me no peace, to such an extent that I could neither sleep nor eat nor do anything else. My strength grew utterly exhausted, and my skin stuck to my bones. All the efforts of skilled physicians were of no avail at all. I went abroad [81] for a cure, but after trying it for six months, I was not benefited in the slightest degree, and those torturing apparitions grew steadily worse and worse. I was brought home again more dead than alive. I went through the horrors and tortures of hell in fullest measure. I had proof then that hell exists, and I knew what it meant! (R.M. French, 30)

To save himself, he acknowledged his sins, repented, confessed and set free all his servants. He humbled himself in poverty and became the lowest type of servant. After he committed himself to his new life, the tormenting apparitions vanished. He made peace with God and understood paradise and recognized how the Kingdom of God is revealed in our hearts. He left his native land fifteen years before, begged in the name of Christ and yet, despite poverty, he knew bliss, happiness and peace. From the torments of hell, he was brought to God's Kingdom by the mercy of the holy Intercessor – Jesus Christ.

    The husband mailed the letter to the man's son and also kept a copy and tucked it inside his Bible. The man wrote the letter to his son with a father's love, with the hope that these last words would serve as a lesson in the son's life – to always remember God, to not scorn the poor and homeless, to know that his father found peace and tranquility for his tormented soul only in poverty and pilgrimage.

Some people may question if this is a true story, if people really make decisions like this. And, the answer is, certainly, yes – even though I do not think it is as visible and noticeable today in the United States of America as in other lands or at other times. Fools for Christ were seen often in Russia. People like the prince, turned beggar are rare, but they do exist. Pain and struggle add depth to the soul. The most interesting people are the ones who have faced adversity and overcome. We may not want pain and struggle, but it builds character. We all want to live the easy life, but the more struggle, the deeper the soul. This is a hard truth.

Not all pilgrims were as good intentioned as our pilgrim. There were pilgrims who had nothing better to do or who were too lazy to work, and they sometimes caused trouble. However, the husband welcomed troublemaking pilgrims who entered his guest house. He and his wife tended to welcome the troublemakers even more than others and urged them to stay longer. Among the kind brethren of Christ, they were often reformed. For example, the couple took in a violent drunk who stole, but he stopped drinking because of the encouragement of his fellow beggars, and then he found a job. Our pilgrim praised the household for its wisdom and love as well as praised God's mercy.

During the morning church service, the pilgrim noticed the family who was housing him prayed with tears of joy. Their faces were so radiant that they brought the pilgrim to tears. After church, everyone present – including forty beggars – went to the dining room to eat in silence and tranquility. Our pilgrim noted that in monasteries, monks read from the lives of the saints during meals, and they could do the same. The priest explained he would love to listen but not read because he had no time with so much to do. The pilgrim shuddered because the priest was too busy to read or study and that he had long since forgotten even what he learned at seminary. The wife explained that the priest was being humble, that he was righteous and kind with many responsibilities. The pilgrim liked the wife's words about the priest. He believed the kind of person one is will determine what he thinks of others. He who has genuine love and prayer loves all equally and does not judge them. Then, the husband acted graciously toward a blind beggar by feeding him. The meal ended when an old woman suddenly became ill. The husband and his wife lay her down on the bed. He went to fetch the doctor, while the rest departed.

The pilgrim explained that, at that moment, he needed to pray. He reflected on peace and quiet and inner prayer. He said,

> I felt as it were hungry for prayer, an urgent need to pour out my soul in prayer, and I had not been in quiet nor alone for forty-eight hours. I felt as though there were in my heart a sort of flood struggling to burst out and flow through all my limbs. To hold it back caused me severe, even if comforting, pain in the heart, a pain that needed to be calmed and satisfied in the silence of prayer. And now I saw why those who really practice interior self-acting prayer have fled from the company of men and hidden themselves in unknown places. I saw further why the venerable Isaiah the Solitary called even the most spiritual and helpful talk mere idle chatter if there were too much of it, just as Ephrem the Syrian says, 'Good speech is silver, but silence is pure gold.' (R.M. French, 32)

The blind beggar who was fed by the husband during dinner practiced the special activity of praying the Jesus Prayer. In the blind beggar's story, we hear further about peasant life, and at this point, we should be aware of the pervasiveness of illiteracy and the power of possessing the skills of reading and writing. There is a great quote the blind beggar remembered reading – before he lost his sight when he was a tailor – about unceasing prayer. He explained to the pilgrim,

> I picked up one of the books, opened it at random, and read, as I remember to this very hour, the following words: "Ceaseless prayer is to call upon the name of God always, whether a man is conversing, or sitting down, or walking, or making something, or eating, whatever he may be doing, in all places and at all times, he ought to call upon God's name." Reading that started me thinking how simple that would be for me. I began to say the prayer in a whisper while I was sewing, and I liked it. (R.M. French, 32)

This is an excellent summary of what it means to pray unceasingly. After the beggar began to practice the Jesus Prayer, a physical manifestation took place as he began to pray only with his tongue, which would form the words on its own. The beggar became blind from "dark water" – also known as glaucoma. The pilgrim knew the quote the blind man recited, and he read it back to him. The blind man requested from the pilgrim to keep reading, and he asked the pilgrim what it means to pray with the heart. They agreed to an arrangement that they would travel together, and the pilgrim would read to the blind man about the prayer of the heart while they walked. The two men thanked their hosts and set out on foot. They walked a bit then sat to read from the *Philokalia*. The pilgrim taught the blind man the technique or method about how to practice interior prayer of the heart. The pilgrim explained,

> When we had read what we needed from the *Philokalia*, he eagerly begged me actually to show him the way the mind finds the heart, how to bring the divine name of Jesus Christ into it, and how to find the joy of praying inwardly with the heart. And I told him all about it thus: "Now you, as a blind man, can see nothing. Yet as a matter of fact you can imagine with your mind and picture to yourself what you have seen in time past, such as a man or some object or other, or one of your own limbs. For instance, can you not picture your hand or your foot as clearly as if you were looking [90] at it? Can you not turn your eyes to it and fix them upon it, blind as they are?'
>
> "'Yes, I can,' he answered.
>
> "'Then picture to yourself your heart in just the same way, turn your eyes to it just as though you were looking at it through your breast, and picture it as clearly as you can. And with your ears listen closely to its beating, beat by beat. When you have got into the way of doing this, begin to fit the words of the prayer to the beats of the heart one after

the other, looking at it all the time. Thus, with the first beat, say or think "Lord," with the second, "Jesus," with the third, "Christ," with the fourth, "have mercy," and with the fifth "on me." And do it over and over again. This will come easily to you, for you already know the groundwork and the first part of praying with the heart. Afterward, when you have grown used to what I have just told you about, you must begin bringing the whole prayer of Jesus into and out of your heart in time with your breathing, as the Fathers taught. Thus, as you draw your breath in, say, or imagine yourself saying, "Lord Jesus Christ," and as you breathe again, "have mercy on me." Do this as often and as much as you can, and in a short space of time you will feel a slight and not unpleasant pain in your heart, followed by a warmth. Thus by God's help you will get the joy of self-acting inward prayer of the heart. But then, whatever you do, be on your guard against imagination and any sort of visions. Don't accept any of them whatever, for the holy Fathers lay down most strongly that inward prayer should be kept free from visions, lest one fall into temptation.' (R.M. French, 33)

From practicing interior prayer of the heart, the blind man felt an intense warmth and an indescribably pleasant sensation in his heart. He had a desire to devote himself to this prayer, a love for Jesus Christ and a vision of a light. Plus, his heart seemed to him as a strong flame that illuminated him. A supernatural activity took place in the blind man. The light made it possible for him to see things even at a great distance. He saw a church burning and the belfry collapse. They arrived at the city of Tobolsk, and it was true. Because of the fulfillment of his vision, the blind man was filled with love for and gratefulness to the Lord Jesus Christ who manifests His grace to sinners. He thanked the pilgrim for teaching him the work of the heart.

According to the pilgrim, the soul in us possess power that is not bound by space and matter. It can see events through darkness and distance. The soul in us is prevented from possessing its greatest capabilities because we suppress it beneath the bonds of our bodies or confused thoughts. We find the truest fulfillment and exercise the highest powers of our souls when we focus on our inner self – away from the external – and when we refine our minds. The pilgrim learned from his starets that all types of people are able to see and sense extraordinary things, but that does not necessarily represent God's grace and could occur as natural manifestations. However, the inexpressible delight from prayer of the heart is a result of God's grace.

The pilgrim experienced personal marvels from the prayer of the heart that included feeling like no one could be happier than him – as if the Kingdom of Heaven could not be greater. Everything around him was more beautiful and blessed in the Name of Jesus Christ. He felt as if he were floating through the air and marveled at the creation of his Creator. He felt like a crowned king and wished to die soon to thank God and be with Him in eternity.

However, at this point, the pilgrim also encountered spiritual struggles, such as anxiety and fear in his heart as well as clouds of thoughts that descended upon his mind. After struggling for a while, he responded by beginning to pray more earnestly, which banished his spiritual struggles completely. He believed everything had been prepared directly by God's hidden guidance and felt more joyous than before.

After walking for a month and then two days of rain, the pilgrim finally found human habitation. He encountered a drunk old man – wearing a military overcoat – who was the post office's postmaster. He offered the pilgrim a drink of liquor, and then we learn an interesting bit of information about the pilgrim – that he had never had a drink in his entire life. Next, in the company of others, while eating dinner, the postmaster and his young female peasant cook got into a fight. After the cook made a bed for the pilgrim, an accident took place. The entire window of the house came showering down with a frightful crash. Two coach drivers entered the hut carrying a bloody man who was a king's messenger.

He washed his wound with water and wine, then galloped away because he had no time to be sick. That night, the pilgrim managed to get some sleep, and in the morning, he thanked God for delivering him from an impending disaster.

Six years later, the pilgrim stopped in a women's monastery, and one of the nuns was the female cook from the post office. She went out of her mind, in shock from terror, and mad from fear because of the terrible crash through the window. However, she was healed by entering the monastery.

This chain of events – where one incident is connected to the next – comes to an end here. Remember, the pilgrim was telling these stories to his spiritual father who inquired while the pilgrim was ready to depart for Jerusalem with an old deaf traveling companion. To be clear, the pilgrim traveled with two different old men. The one was blind – who the pilgrim met during the hospitality of the pious couple who had a guesthouse for the poor – and they talked about prayer together as they walked to Tobolsk. The other was deaf – who the pilgrim planned to travel with to Jerusalem – as was mentioned at the beginning of the Fourth Narrative. Also, there was one starets who died and reappeared in dreams. And, one spiritual father who the pilgrim met during his journey and to whom he was telling stories.

The pilgrim began to tell a new story to his spiritual father. In the story, the pilgrim attended a church service and the priest – who was a young man but frightfully thin and pale – invited him to lunch. The young, thin, pale priest performed the church service quite slowly because he loved to reflect on every word of a prayer to benefit from the inner experience and interior life of prayer. When the pilgrim asked how to attain a spiritually enlightened interior life, the priest explained one must take the Holy Scriptures and focus all one's attention and meditate on it. Same with a prayer. One must repeat the prayer frequently for long periods of time.

Then, as the pilgrim was sitting in the kitchen reading the *Philokalia*, an old woman in the corner was unceasingly whispering the Jesus Prayer. She made a habit of praying the Jesus Prayer since she was a little girl. The woman was once arranged in marriage, and the day before the wedding, her bridegroom died, which frightened her and led her to celibacy as well as visiting distant shrines and praying to God. She was kept safe during her travels because of unceasingly repeating the Jesus Prayer. As the woman grew old and infirm, she was helped by the young, thin, pale priest.

According to the pilgrim, the surest and quickest way to acquire the fruits of the Jesus Prayer is by the frequency and duration of repeating it.

In the pilgrim's next story, he struck up a conversation in the evening with a man who had a coachman, horses and carriage. The man was a high-ranking captain in the navy. He retired because, as he grew older, he developed gout, an incurable infirmity. His wife was extravagant and played cards. She cleaned him out and left him. He was left alone with his eight-year-old godson. The boy was a mischief-maker. The man got the boy to settle down by ordering him to repeat continuously the Jesus Prayer, and if he stopped, the man would show the boy a rod to frighten him. The Jesus Prayer affected the boy, and he became quieter and better than before. Plus, the boy developed an irresistible desire to pray unceasingly. When the man and boy moved away, the boy was unhappy because when others would play, it prevented him from praying. So, the boy decided to return home on his own. Then, the boy was found dead in his empty house, lying on the floor with his hands devoutly folded on his chest. The boy's return home was quite astonishing because of the quickness of his return – traveling about sixty-five miles a day, which is not possible without God's specific providence and care for him. Considering the power of prayer in their lives, the old man concluded that he had not attained the measure of prayer that the boy acquired. When the pilgrim told the man about the *Philokalia*, the man was pleased to accept the advice and promised to obtain a copy for himself. The pilgrim made a beautiful connection between the boy, the discipline of the rod and all of us who are learning to pray. The pilgrim explained that the rod taught the boy to pray and he acquired consolation. Perhaps, the grief and sufferings that we encounter are God's own rods. Our Heavenly Father, Who is filled with boundless love, teaches us with these rods to be more attentive to prayer leading us to inexpressible consolation.

With that, the pilgrim finished telling stories to his spiritual father, as he was about to travel to Jerusalem. The pilgrim's spiritual father left him with a beautiful blessing – that the all-loving grace of God shed its light on his path and go with him, as the angel Raphael went with Tobias.

Conclusion

The Pilgrim

The pilgrim had a genuine character. As we got to know him, he became a friend. He was honest, sincere and fully devoted to encountering God through prayer. He knew he was a sinner, but he was in search of and committed to the higher aspects of human possibility. His experiences were unique and different from ours, but it is possible to see ourselves in him. We can relate to him. Sometimes, he was what we yearn to be. Is he a saint? Perhaps. Perhaps not. Like him, we all have that potential. Each of us could, perhaps, become a saint. It is possible. Theosis is attainable for all faithful Christians. The pilgrim earnestly sought truth, and as we journeyed with him, he became our teacher. He desired Salvation and was on the path to union with God. His goal was to reach a higher spiritual existence. As I read his story, I realized that life is truly an adventure. I learned that we do not need a lot of money to live adventurous lives. Road trips, hiking and cookouts are within everyone's reach. The pilgrim encountered many people, but he prized solitude and enjoyed being on his own. He took the road less traveled and the unbeaten path – physically by walking through Russia as well as in a spiritual sense. He had entered through the narrow gate that leads to life, as Jesus taught. With his boldness and courage, he was our protagonist and hero. His adventures were filled with adversity, but he moved forward. We cheered for him as we read. And that quality adds to the book's status as a literary classic. He was the kind of individual that a person will not soon forget. But, this book is more than a literary classic because this book is also clear, direct and precise instruction on how to pray unceasingly. The story and lessons together make it a masterpiece. The pilgrim ended up being an excellent vehicle to teach us about the Jesus Prayer, which if we try to master for ourselves, it will take us on our own adventures and, hopefully, to union with God. The pilgrim may be the main character, but the story is nothing without the Jesus Prayer. *The Way of a Pilgrim* is a great story filled treasure that can enrich our spiritual lives.

The more times I read it, the more I find myself enjoying it. I hope you have developed a similar sentiment.

Theosis and Hesychia

The Way of a Pilgrim reminds us that we are all pilgrims on a journey to God, and it provides comfort and support as we make our way to theosis (deification, divinization – being made divine) and our Heavenly Father. In *The Orthodox Church* (229-231), Bishop Ware provided six accessible points to clarify the understanding of theosis (he used the word deification). One, deification is possible for the normal Christian, for every Christian, for all Christians. The process of deification begins now here on earth, but it is attained by few. Two, if a person is deified in this life, he or she still needs to repent. The deified person is still a sinner but continuously prays for mercy – as taught through the Jesus Prayer. Three, the ways or the means in which a person becomes deified are not extraordinary. They include going to church, receiving the sacraments, praying to God, reading the Gospels and following the Commandments with their moral rules. Four, a person cannot be deified without his or her neighbor or if he or she is selfish. We must love God and our neighbors. People can imitate the life of God as Holy Trinity by dwelling in one another for each other.

Five, some down-to-earth actions that manifest deification are praying, caring for the sick, helping the poor and working for others. These are not different ways, but rather are all along the same path. Six, in order to achieve deification, we need the Church, which was appointed by God for our pilgrimage here on earth as we travel to Heaven.

If the requirements for theosis seem like a lot to bear, one should consider the value of theosis and possessing God-like qualities. The price (asceticism, prayer and participation in the Church) for the reward of theosis is little. I can testify that the journey toward theosis is amazing, and I recognize that attaining theosis is the fullest potential and highest possibility for human beings. Theosis is the reward, but it should not be the reason we take action – meaning that we should focus on being faithful servants of our Lord and Savior Jesus Christ. If one follows the path of humble and faithful servant to the Lord, one will be rewarded with theosis.

One fruit of theosis – with the help of the Jesus Prayer – is hesychia, which is a Greek term that translates into stillness or inward silence. In Eastern Orthodox Christianity, those who work for this fruit are typically monastics who are known as hesychasts and the practice is known as hesychasm. Bishop Ware explained, "*Hesychia* signifies concentration combined with inward tranquility" (*The Orthodox Way*, 122). By concentrating on the Jesus Prayer in mind, heart and soul, the hesychast achieves inward tranquility. Eastern Orthodox Christianity teaches that only through prayer – preeminently, the Jesus Prayer – can one achieve inward tranquility. This condition is possible when one is filled in mind, heart and soul with Jesus and the Holy Spirit. As Apostle Paul said, "it is no longer I who live, but Christ who lives in me" (Galatians 2:20, RSV).

As Jesus explained, "If you continue in my word, you are truly my disciples, and you will know the truth, and the truth will make you free" (John 8:31b, RSV). The truth in Jesus's teachings do not make us carefree, so we can be reckless, but rather frees us from bondage to sin, evil, the devil, death and Hell – which is much more valuable than to be without care. The undisciplined human mind, heart and soul are restless. Discipline, asceticism and prayer are spiritual tools that help us calm and strengthen the mind, heart and soul. A disciplined, ascetic and prayerful person will develop a healthy mind, heart and soul. Discursive thinking in a restless person cannot be bullied into tranquility or attacked with pure willpower. However, we must use our wills to develop good habits and train ourselves in discipline, asceticism and prayer. If a person trains his mind, heart and soul to practice the Jesus Prayer, then the person has the potential to taste the fruit of hesychia and experience theosis.

The mind has the power to be a person's great strength and ally; however, as Bishop Ware insightfully pointed out, "The ever-restless mind demands from us some task, so as to satisfy its constant need to be active... The mind needs some task which will keep it busy, and yet enable it to reach out beyond itself into stillness" (*The Orthodox Way*, 122). To attain stillness, the Eastern Orthodox Church prescribes the unceasing practice of the Jesus Prayer.

Psyche

With the help of the Jesus Prayer, my mind constantly reflects on and is connected to our Lord and Savior Jesus Christ. If our minds are continuously filled with prayers to the Lord, there will be no room in our minds for the enemy/the evil one/Satan to disturb us. One's mind should always be mindful of God and guard itself from all influence and temptation of the evil one. The person who can do this will have a healthy, strong and clean psyche.

The word "psyche" is fascinating, complicated and deep. It is familiar to many people knowledgeable of the English language with words like "psychology" and "psychiatry" which conjure up ideas about the mind and mental health. However, the word "psyche" comes from the Greek language where the letter "p" is pronounced, and the word has a much more robust meaning. In Greek, psyche means soul. At some point in the development of the English language, a contributor adopted the Greek word and applied it to reference mental workings. English users ran with it and never looked back to the point that few are aware of the word's origin. We should be aware of the meaning of psyche and the relationship between the mind and the soul. My intention is to help create a bridge across the chasm that distances the mind from the soul as we know them in our secular western world.

Mental health is important. It is just as important as physical health. Being without health is illness and illness leads to death. Many people struggle with mental illness, depression, addiction and drug abuse. These problems are not new. The human condition has not changed. Over 2000 years ago, people certainly dealt with such adversity and attributed it to demons. Today, medication and therapy may be used to battle adversity, but the source of illness remains the evil dwelling inside. Many societies in our current world have secularized themselves and have tried to remove God and Jesus from life. This is foolish and dangerous. Medication and therapy have value, but if a person wants to cleanse oneself from the evil and darkness dwelling within, then the purest remedy is the love, light and truth of our Lord and Savior Jesus Christ. We all must battle our demons, and I hope for the benefit of the world, we all rediscover Jesus Christ and God.

It is essential for the health of one's mind and soul – one's psyche – that one develops a relationship with God. God is Incomprehensible, Infinite and

Eternal; however, we know Him as Heavenly Father and can develop a relationship with Him through His Son Jesus the Christ. Like all important relationships, honest open communication is vital, and we communicate with God through prayer, and since the only way to the Father is the Son, we must develop a relationship with the Son through prayer – hence the importance of the Jesus Prayer.

Heaven and agape love are very real and so are Hell and illness in the mind and soul. We can experience Heaven and Hell in this world, but they are only hints of what it is like in eternity. Jesus can save us from Hell and lead us to Heaven. He is the only one who has this power. As Saint Peter expressed to Jesus, "Lord, to whom [else] shall we go? You have the words of eternal life; and we have believed, and have come to know, that you are the Holy One of God" (John 6:68, RSV). Jesus loves the world so much that he died for it, but we are not worthy of him and his sacrifice. Developing a relationship with Jesus is the only way to Heaven and eternal life – and if you want Heaven and eternal life, you must go to Jesus. Praying the Jesus Prayer is important because Jesus has the power to save.

My hope is that psychology and psychiatry will apply theology to aid the sick and those suffering through the hell of mental illness or addiction. People should be aware that psychiatric medicine can help, but it cannot save. Medication can assist the victim who is going through hellish illness, but only Jesus

Christ can save the victim from the beatings of the devil. Modern medicine is a tool, but not the final solution. Psychological therapy is good, but the Church is better. The Church calls Herself a hospital for the sick, and all of us Christians who are honest with ourselves know the truth of this statement. To climb out of a hellish pit, a person should go to Jesus, His Church and His saints who gained victory over sin, evil, the devil, death and Hell. This is the path to Salvation.

Final Thoughts

This exposition is my humble attempt to affirm the power of unceasing prayer – preeminently, the Jesus Prayer as taught in *The Way of a Pilgrim*. There are other articles and books on prayer that are better than my exposition, and there are certainly greater religious Christians – ascetics, mystics, hesychasts and saints – who have better taught the unceasing practice of the Jesus Prayer and who have accomplished more with it. Even so, prayer is so important that I – as a Professor of Christian Theology – wanted to teach it to my students and write about it for the benefit of my readers. The Jesus Prayer has helped to heal me from many sins as I have struggled in this fallen world, and it has also brought me great joy. I simply wanted to share its power and benefits with you. I pray this work has led you closer to our Heavenly Father. Amen.

Bibliography and Works Cited

The Way of a Pilgrim Analysis:
   When quoting the masterpiece, I cited from...
- French, R.M. (translator). *The Way of a Pilgrim and The Pilgrim Continues His Way.* Internet: https://jbburnett.com/resources/french_way_of_a_pilgrim.pdf. Accessed 12-23-2020.

When summarizing the masterpiece, I paraphrased from...
- Savin, Olga (translator). *The Way of a Pilgrim and The Pilgrim Continues His Way.* Shambhala Classics: 2001.

Introduction and Conclusion:
- Brianchaninov, Bishop Ignatius [Saint]. *On the Prayer of Jesus: The Classic Guide to the Practice of Unceasing Prayer Found in The Way of a Pilgrim.* New Seeds: 2006.
- Hopko, Father Thomas. "Foreword." *The Way of a Pilgrim and The Pilgrim Continues His Way.* Shambhala Classics: 2001.
- Palmer, G. E.H. Sherrard, Philip. Ware, Kallistos. "Introduction." *The Philokalia:*

The Complete Text (Vol. 1). Farrar, Straus and Giroux: 1983.
- Ware, Bishop Kallistos (Timothy). *The Orthodox Church: An Introduction to Eastern Christianity* [New Edition, Third]. Penguin Books: 2015.
- Ware, Bishop Kallistos (Timothy). *The Orthodox Way* [Revised Edition]. St Vladimir's Seminary Press: 1995.
- Ware, Bishop Kallistos (Timothy). "Foreword." *On the Prayer of Jesus: The Classic Guide to the Practice of Unceasing Prayer Found in The Way of a Pilgrim.* New Seeds: 2006.
- Wikipedia.org. *The Way of a Pilgrim.* Accessed 12-23-2020.
- Wikipedia.org. *Jesus Prayer.* Accessed 12-23-2020.
- Wikipedia.org. *Hesychasm.* Accessed 12-23-2020.

Further Reading:
- Elder Joseph [Saint]. *Monastic Wisdom: The Letters of Elder Joseph the Hesychast.* Saint Anthony's Greek Orthodox Monastery: 1998.

www.ingramcontent.com/pod-product-compliance
Lightning Source LLC
LaVergne TN
LVHW051551070426
835507LV00021B/2516